THE CASE FOR
FREEWILL
THEISM

A PHILOSOPHICAL
ASSESSMENT

DAVID BASINGER

This book is a gift from the
RICHARD GRAY FAMILY to
Bethany College

InterVarsity Press
Downers Grove, Illinois

InterVarsity Press® is the book-publishing division of InterVarsity Christian Fellowship®, a student movement active on campus at hundreds of universities, colleges and schools of nursing in the United States of America, and a member movement of the International Fellowship of Evangelical Students. For information about local and regional activities, write Public Relations Dept., InterVarsity Christian Fellowship, 6400 Schroeder Rd., P.O. Box 7895, Madison, WI 53707-7895.

All Scripture quotations, unless otherwise indicated, are taken from the HOLY BIBLE, NEW INTERNATIONAL VERSION®. NIV®. Copyright ©1973, 1978, 1984 by International Bible Society. Used by permission of Zondervan Publishing House. All rights reserved.

ISBN 0-8308-1876-6

Printed in the United States of America ♾

Library of Congress Cataloging-in-Publication Data

Basinger, David.
  The case for freewill theism: a philosophical assessment/David
Basinger.
    p.   cm.
  Includes bibliographical references.
  ISBN 0-8308-1876-6 (pbk.: alk. paper)
  1. Theism. 2. Freewill and determinism—Religious aspects.
I. Title.
BL200.B33 1996
211'.34—dc20   96-19420
                                                                CIP

21	20	19	18	17	16	15	14	13	12	11	10	9	8	7	6	5	4	3	2	1
13	12	11	10	09	08	07	06	05	04	03	02	01	00	99	98	97	96			

Acknowledgments

Some of the material in this book first appeared (in more or less modified form) in previous publications of mine. Specifically, I have utilized material from the following articles and books:

"In What Sense Must God Be Omnibenevolent?" *International Journal for the Philosophy of Religion* 14 (1983).

"In What Sense Must God Do His Best? A Response to Hasker," *International Journal for the Philosophy of Religion* 18 (1985).

"Middle Knowledge and Divine Control: Some Clarifications," *International Journal for the Philosophy of Religion* 30 (1991).

"Practical Implications," in Clark Pinnock et al., *The Openness of God* (Downers Grove, Ill.: InterVarsity Press, 1994).

"Petitionary Prayer: A Response to Murray and Meyers," *Religious Studies* 31 (1995).

"Human Freedom and Divine Providence: Some New Thoughts on an Old Problem," *Religious Studies* 15 (1979).

"Middle Knowledge and Classical Christian Thought," *Religious Studies* 22 (1986).

"Plantinga, Pluralism and Justified Religious Belief," *Faith and Philosophy* 8 (January 1991).

"Simple Foreknowledge and Providential Control," *Faith and Philosophy* 10 (July 1993).

"Divine Control and Human Freedom: Is Middle Knowledge the Answer?" *Journal of the Evangelical Theological Society* 36 (1993).

"Can an Evangelical Christian Justifiably Deny God's Knowledge of the Future?" *Christian Scholar's Review* 25 (December 1995).

All materials are used with permission.

Preface

Is this the best of all possible worlds? If not, why did God create *this* world when so many other options were open to him? Can God intervene in this world? If he can, to what extent does he do so? Does he help us secure jobs or admission to college? Can we initiate such intervention by prayer? Or is his activity much more general in scope? If God can and does intervene in our world, what should we say when a child is born with a physical or mental abnormality, when a volcano kills over twenty thousand people, or when starvation takes the lives of millions? Are these occurrences part of God's will? Or does God, as much as we, wish that such things did not occur?

The primary purpose of this book is to outline the manner in which proponents of one important theological perspective, which I label "freewill theism," conceive of the relationship between God and the world and thus respond (or at least attempt to respond) to questions such as these.

This book is the culmination of many years' work. I wish to thank the administration of Roberts Wesleyan College for granting me a sabbatical that freed me from my responsibilities as a college teacher and allowed me to bring this material together into its present form. Also, I wish to acknowledge the profound influence of my brother Randall, with whom I have been in constructive dialogue regarding the issues covered in this work for the last twenty years.

Introduction

Until quite recently, most philosophers of religion grouped mono-
theists into two basic categories: those who believe God to be a
personal, omnipotent, omniscient, perfectly good being and those
who do not.[1] It was always acknowledged that theists in the former
category differed somewhat in their understanding of the exact
nature of the divine attributes. But it was assumed that enough
homogeneity in thought existed to warrant treating such theists as
a group when addressing important questions concerning God's
existence and his providential relationship with our world (e.g.,
evil, prayer, miracles or divine guidance).

But there is a growing consensus among philosophers of religion that theists who believe God to be a personal, omnipotent,
omniscient, perfectly good being are best divided into three categories that are based on three distinct understandings of God's
capacity to control earthly affairs.[2]

Process theists maintain that God is omnipotent in the sense that
he has all the power it is possible for a being to possess, but they

deny that such power includes even the *capacity* to unilaterally bring about any state of affairs. Rather, as they see it, all entities always possess some power of self-determination, and thus all reality is always cocreative.[3]

Theological determinists, at the other end of the spectrum, do not deny that God has created a world containing individuals who exercise voluntary choice (who possess freedom of choice) and that such choice is the immediate cause for much that occurs in our world. They contend, though, that God has the capacity to control the natural order unilaterally and that God can unilaterally ensure that all individuals will always voluntarily make the exact decisions he would have them make. Thus he is considered ultimately in control of all earthly affairs. God may use human decision-making and/or the natural order to accomplish his purposes, but neither is viewed in any sense as keeping God from accomplishing exactly what he intends to accomplish.[4]

Another group of theists, increasingly labeled *freewill theists*,[5] disagree with both process theists and theological determinists. Unlike process theists, freewill theists acknowledge that God can unilaterally intervene in earthly affairs and does so at times. But they deny that God can both grant individuals freedom and control its use. Unlike theological determinists, they maintain that God has voluntarily given up complete control of earthly affairs to the extent that he has voluntarily granted humanity freedom.[6]

To express this taxonomy of perspectives even more succinctly, theists who believe that God is a personal, omnipotent, omniscient, perfectly good being can be distinguished as follows: those who believe that God can never unilaterally ensure that what occurs is that which he would have occur (process theists), those who believe that God always does so (theological determinists) and those who believe that God chooses at times to give up control (freewill theists).

The purpose of this book, as the title indicates, is to subject freewill theism (FWT) to a philosophical assessment. But what exactly does this mean, and why do I believe it to be a worthwhile project? FWT, as I understand it, is best characterized as a set of related beliefs about the nature of reality, that is, about the way the world is.[7] However, such beliefs can be assessed in at least two ways. We can attempt to determine whether the world (i.e., reality) actually is as described in a belief. That is, we can attempt to determine whether the world actually is as a person holding a belief thinks it is. This is ontological assessment. Or we can attempt to determine whether (or to what extent) a person is justified in believing that the world really is the way he or she believes it is. This is epistemic assessment.[8] In this book I mainly subject FWT to *epistemic* belief assessment. I will at times comment on the ontological status of the beliefs held by freewill theists (i.e., discuss whether these beliefs are actually true). But my primary goal is to determine what freewill theists can or cannot justifiably maintain about the nature of reality.[9]

To be even more specific, to affirm *basic* freewill theism (BFWT), as I will be using this phrase, is to hold that since God cannot control voluntary human choice, the fact that he has granted humanity significant, pervasive freedom of choice means that he has voluntarily given up total control over much of what occurs in the earthly realm. No freewill theist, however, affirms only BFWT. All hold additional beliefs about God's nature and how God relates to earthly affairs, beliefs that at points not only differ from freewill theist to freewill theist but are sometimes even incompatible. Accordingly, an epistemic assessment of BFWT can concern itself with at least two distinct questions. Are freewill theists justified in affirming BFWT (i.e., in believing that God's decision to grant humans freedom has limited his control over earthly affairs)? And assuming that freewill theists are justified in affirming BFWT, what else can (or cannot) be inferred about the nature of reality?

I will discuss to some extent whether BFWT itself can be affirmed. But my main goal in this book is to determine what (else) can or cannot coherently be maintained about God's nature and his relationship with earthly affairs by a person who is a proponent of BFWT. More specifically, my goal is to determine what a person who affirms BFWT can (or should or must) say about God's omniscience and goodness, the origin of and reason for evil, and the efficacy of prayer.

Summary of Chapters

In chapter one I outline in greater detail the relationship between God and the world that is envisioned by freewill theists, contrasting it with the relationships proposed by theological determinists and process theists.

Chapter two is concerned with the important relationship between BFWT and God's knowledge. Some theists maintain that God infallibly knows only that which *has* occurred and *is* occurring—that God possesses only what I call "present knowledge."[10] Others hold that God also knows all that *will* occur (from our perspective) in the actual world—that he possesses "simple foreknowledge." And still others hold that God also knows what *would* in fact happen in every possible situation, including what every possible free creature would do in every possible situation in which that creature could find itself—that God possesses "middle knowledge."

I first consider the type(s) of knowledge that the God of BFWT can be said to possess. Some philosophers (most notably William Hasker) have argued that no one (including no freewill theist) can justifiably maintain that God possesses middle knowledge. Others have argued that a freewill theist must maintain, at the very least, that God possesses simple foreknowledge. I argue that although a freewill theist need not affirm any specific model of omniscience, no philosopher has yet successfully demonstrated that a freewill theist is prohibited from affirming any of them.

I also consider the exact relationship between these three models of omniscience and God's providential activity. Everyone agrees that a God with middle knowledge—a God who knew before creation, for instance, exactly what would occur, given every creative option—has more providential control over earthly affairs than a God who possesses only present knowledge—who does not even know infallibly at present all that will occur in any world containing free creatures. But what of a God with simple foreknowledge? Does such a God have more providential control over earthly affairs than a God with present knowledge alone? I argue that he does not, and thus that the question whether God possesses middle knowledge is a very important one for freewill theists to answer.

The purpose of chapter three is to identify the moral principles that freewill theists can or cannot reasonably maintain guide God's thinking as God determines what he would have come about in our world. I argue that freewill theists, especially those who believe that God possesses middle knowledge, *can* consider God to be under a number of creative obligations, for example, the obligation to create (or attempt to create) the "best" possible world or a world that contains no unrecompensed suffering or a world in which our lives are on the whole worth living or a world in which value for all is maximized to the extent possible. I conclude, though, that there is nothing inherent in BFWT (or theism in general) that *requires* freewill theists to consider God to be under any such obligation.

Chapter four assesses the relationship between BFWT and evil. Can freewill theists maintain that this world contains no excess evil—no evil that an all powerful, perfectly good being could and would prohibit? Or do the types and amounts of evil that we experience present an insurmountable problem? After clarifying the exact nature of the question, I consider in detail the inductive challenge that evil is said to pose to BFWT, namely, that the types and amount of evil we experience render unjustified the belief that this world contains no excess evil and thus render unjustified the belief that the God of BFWT exists. I conclude that, while critics such as William Rowe and David Griffin can themselves coherently deny that the existence of the God of BFWT is compatible with the evil in our world, freewill theists can coherently disagree.

In chapter five I consider the relationship between BFWT and petitionary prayer. All theists (e.g., all theological determinists, process theists and freewill theists) believe prayer to be an important, efficacious theistic activity. As I point out, however, only the freewill theist can maintain that divine intervention is at times dependent on whether we ask for God's assistance. I also note, though, that given the freewill theist's commitment to a world in which God values free human decision-making and thus normally allows the natural order to proceed, the freewill theist cannot reasonably assume that petitionary prayer actually does often initiate unilateral divine activity.

Epistemic Context

It is important that I attempt to place my overall strategy in its proper epistemic context. The primary goal in this book, as noted, is to determine what additional beliefs can (or cannot) be affirmed by a proponent of BFWT. Thus my discussion is quite "defensive" in the sense that it is primarily concerned with whether freewill theists can avoid the charge that they affirm beliefs that are false, incoherent or incompossible with other beliefs. And I make no apology for this, because such analysis, as I see it, is not only important but utterly necessary if we are to assess BFWT appropriately.

However, I want to distance myself from proponents of what I label "bunker theology," who believe not only that it is necessary for a theist to be able to defend her beliefs from external attack but also that this is *all* that is necessary. As they see it, a theist fulfills her epistemic duties with respect to her religious beliefs when she demonstrates that these beliefs can withstand external attack, that is, demonstrates that the affirmation of these beliefs cannot be shown to be unjustified. She need not engage in positive apologetics (consider positive evidence for her beliefs). Only "negative apologetics," the refutation of challenges, is required.[11]

It seems to me, however, that the existence of pervasive religious diversity, the fact that seemingly knowledgeable epistemic peers affirm different, sometimes contradictory, religious beliefs, renders this perspective unacceptable. It is not, as I see it, that the existence of such diversity necessarily renders belief in any given religious perspective unacceptable. Consider, by way of illustration, an analogous situation. Tom and Bill, students in the same introductory philosophy class, are discussing a forthcoming exam. Tom believes the exam is on Friday, while Bill believes it to be on the following Monday. Before they talked, neither had any reason to doubt that he was correct. Both were in class when the exam date was announced, and neither had any reason to doubt his auditory faculties or memory. Moreover, each remains convinced he is right. So what should they conclude?

It would be improper, it seems to me, for either Bill or Tom to assume immediately that his belief can no longer be considered true. And the same, I maintain, holds with respect to the pervasive disagreements among religious perspectives. It is an undeniable fact that seemingly sincere, knowledgeable theists often find themselves affirming incompatible religious beliefs. However, this fact alone is not a sufficient reason for a proponent of any given religious perspective to assume immediately that her religious beliefs must be abandoned.

We all know from experience, though, that conflicts between beliefs can sometimes be resolved. To return to our classroom scenario, further investigation might uncover that Tom's (or Bill's) hearing was unreliable on the day in question because he had an ear infection or was taking a prescription drug that had affected his hearing and/or memory. Or Tom and Bill could probably resolve their conflict simply by contacting the instructor. Accordingly, *if their goal is to discover the truth,* it appears that they are under a prima facie obligation to do what can be done to resolve their conflict.

The same, I believe, holds with respect to conflicting religious beliefs. It is true that the reality of pervasive religious diversity is not in and of itself a sufficient reason for any given theist to abandon her beliefs. But it does not follow from this fact that the theist who becomes aware of pervasive religious diversity can therefore dismiss further consideration of this phenomenon. Epistemic conflicts between believers can sometimes be resolved. Thus, as I see it, *if the goal of a theist (or a person studying religious belief) is to maximize truth and minimize error,* she is under a prima facie obligation to attempt to resolve such conflicts.

Moreover, while students may not always be interested in determining exactly when an exam is scheduled to be given, most theists (and nontheists) do claim to be interested in affirming truth and avoiding error. Thus the existence of pervasive diversity—the fact that seemingly sincere, knowledgeable individuals continue to affirm incompatible religious beliefs—does, I believe, place the knowledgeable theist under the type of prima facie epistemic obligation in question.

It must be emphasized that such an obligation is only prima facie. There may be many legitimate reasons that it cannot be discharged immediately (or ever). A given theist, for example, may not have the time or resources to investigate further. Furthermore, I do not believe that the mere existence of this obligation need have any immediate bearing on the epistemic status of a theist's beliefs. Of course, a theist who becomes aware of religious diversity may find herself less inclined to affirm certain beliefs. And information uncovered during an attempt to resolve the conflict in question may well lead a theist to believe that she is now less (or more) justified in affirming her religious beliefs than she was initially. However, the mere recognition of the existence of the obligation in question does not itself require a theist to modify her epistemic attitude toward her beliefs.

It is my belief, though, that once the theist acknowledges the reality of pervasive religious diversity, she can no longer justifiably choose to retain a purely defensive posture. That is, I deny that a knowledgeable theist can reasonably conclude that she is under no further obligation simply because the existence of pervasive diversity does not require that she abandon her beliefs. If she desires to determine the truth of the matter to the extent possible, she is obligated, in principle, to engage in further investigation. The arena of positive apologetics must at least be entered. The game of "negative apologetics" will no longer be sufficient.

To state this important point differently yet, it is my contention that, given pervasive diversity, it not enough for a theist simply to defend her perspective, although this is a perfectly proper and necessary activity. She is also under an epistemic obligation to determine which of the competing perspectives she ought to attempt to defend. She ought, in other words, to look for reasons why her perspective is worthy of being defended.

But what if attempts to resolve the challenge of diversity by objectively considering all the relevant data prove unsuccessful (as I personally believe will be the case)? That is, what if a theist can discover no objective basis by which she can determine which of the competing belief systems is more worthy of affirmation? Is there some way she can at least decide the issue for herself?[12] I believe the answer is yes. If a theist who has comparatively analyzed the various competing sets of religious (and nonreligious) truth claims in an attempt to resolve the challenge of diversity has not uncovered any compelling objective basis for deciding the issue, then I believe that she is justified in resolving the conflict in her favor by an appeal to personal preference. That is, at this point I believe she is justified in resolving the conflict in her favor by appealing to her feeling (intuition, noetic belief) that the set of basic religious truth claims she affirms better organizes and explains the relevant components of reality than any other.

This means that I ultimately arrive at an epistemic position quite similar in some important respects to the one affirmed by the proponent of bunker theology. We both deny that there exists an objective basis for demonstrating conclusively that a given worldview (metaphysical conceptualization of reality) is correct.[13] We both emphasize the importance of being able to defend one's perspective from external attack. But unlike the proponent of bunker theology, I contend that the knowledgeable theist is, in principle, justified in "playing defense" *only if* she has considered seriously the reasons that can be offered for affirming the competing belief systems and has found hers to be most compelling personally.[14]

Conclusion

This, then, is the context in which my assessment of BFWT must be placed. I conclude that freewill theists can justifiably affirm not only BFWT but also most of the additional beliefs they desire to affirm. However, my main reason for undertaking this assessment is *not* to help freewill theists more safely "hunker down into their bunkers." My goal is to help those interested in considering the various theistic options to better understand the beliefs to which freewill theists (or more properly, proponents of BFWT) are committed, and thus to be in a better position to determine whether this metaphysical perspective (worldview) is in fact worthy of serious consideration.

1
BASIC
FREEWILL
THEISM

THERE ARE MANY DIFFERENT WAYS TO CONCEIVE OF THE RELA-
tionship between God and the world. *Pantheists* make no distinction. They identify God with the eternal, impersonal world
system. *Deists* distinguish God from the world, but their God
functions as a creator and designer only. They deny that God
has a continued personal interest and involvement in the world.
Finitists distinguish between God and the world and believe
that God involves himself personally in earthly affairs. However, they deny that God is all powerful, all knowing and/or
perfectly good.[1]

Freewill theists fall into none of these categories.[2] Rather, they
are proponents of what William Rowe calls "standard theism,"
which maintains not only that God and the world are distinct and
that God interacts with the world but also that God is omnipotent,
omniscient and perfectly good.[3] Standard theists differ on many
points, for example, the exact nature of God's knowledge and the
moral obligations under which God functions. But what differen-
tiates freewill theists from other standard theists is primarily their

perspective on the nature of God's power, especially as it relates to the question, To what extent, if any, can God unilaterally control earthly affairs?

Process Theism

Some standard theists, usually labeled *process theists*, believe that all entities, "human" and "nonhuman" alike, possess some degree of self-determination in the sense that they "have some power to determine themselves and to influence other things."[4] As they see it, God does continually present to every entity at every moment the optimum real possibility open to it, and every entity does in fact feel some compulsion (urge, attraction) to act in accordance with God's lure. However, because every entity possesses some power of self-determination, God can *never* ensure that what he has determined should occur will in fact occur, even in what we identify as the natural realm. Rather, God's purposes for all entities "always require the cooperation of [these entities] for their realization."[5]

To state this in somewhat more tangible terms, the relationship between the God of process theism and the world can be compared to the relationship between a conductor and her orchestra. Without the orchestra the conductor could not express herself (after all, she plays no instrument). Without the conductor there would be no unified musical performance. Moreover, the conductor, no matter how competent, cannot unilaterally guarantee that the piece will be played exactly as she has decided that it should be played. The most that she can expect is that her influence will be present. The extent to which what she has envisioned is actualized is determined by the ability and responsiveness of those playing the instruments.[6]

And so it is with the God of process theism and his "orchestra." Although God does identify and does share with all relevant entities that which he has determined should occur in every situation, there is no guarantee from the process perspective that what has been identified as the best option will in fact ever come about. God can only *hope* that what he has envisioned will occur; there can be no assurance. God is at every moment taking a risk and is subject to surprise. Accordingly, the process answer to the question at hand is clear. Since God cannot unilaterally bring about any state of affairs in our world, God *cannot* unilaterally guarantee to *any* extent that what he has determined should occur in our world will in fact come about.[7]

Freewill theists disagree with process theists on this important point. They fall into the group of standard theists, usually labeled *classical theists*, who believe that God can, at least to *some* extent, unilaterally guarantee that what occurs in this world is what he has determined should occur.

Classical Theism

Classical theists agree on a number of issues related to God's power. Historically, a few classical theists have actually claimed that God can bring about absolutely any state of affairs, even that which is logically impossible.[8] However, the vast majority at present agree with Thomas V. Morris that "to say that God is so powerful that he can do the logically impossible is not pious or reverential; it is just confused."[9] For classical theists today, to say that God is omnipotent is to say, roughly speaking, that God can bring about any state of affairs that it is not logically impossible for him to bring about.[10]

What, though, is it logically impossible for God to bring about? Classical theists agree that God cannot bring about any state of affairs that could not possibly exist under any set of conditions. They agree, for instance, that God cannot create square circles or married bachelors, since there can be no such things.[11] Moreover, they agree that God cannot bring about any set of possible states of affairs that cannot occur simultaneously—that are not *compos-*

sible. For example, although there may be possible conditions under which a person would die at the age of two and possible conditions under which this person would live to marry at the age of twenty-five, classical theists deny that it is possible for God to create a world in which the same person both dies at two and marries at twenty-five. These states of affairs are not compossible.[12] Few, if any, classical theists, however, believe that God desires to bring about something that is self-contradictory or incompossible; thus classical theists do not view this "limitation" as in any significant sense negatively affecting God's ability to actualize unilaterally his creative goals—his ability to ensure that what occurs is what he would have occur. They view this limitation, rather, as simply one aspect of the metaphysical framework within which God must *always* function.[13]

Classical theists also acknowledge that God has created and is sustaining an impersonal natural order—animate and inanimate natural objects and the laws that govern their activity—and that this order functions to some extent independently of him. For instance, such things as seasonal changes or the birth of a baby are often attributed in part to the orderly outworking of the natural patterns that God has established. However, classical theists deny that nature has a will of its own. They believe that God possesses the power to modify or to circumvent any natural process at any time. Consequently they deny that the existence of this natural realm, in and of itself, places any additional limitations on God's ability to control earthly affairs. As they see it, the only limitation on God's power in a world that contained only impersonal natural objects governed by impersonal natural laws would be his inability to bring about states of affairs that were intrinsically impossible or incompossible.

Classical theists do, though, uniformly maintain that God is not the only entity exercising efficacious voluntary choice (decision-making). That is, they maintain that God is not the only entity voluntarily (freely) making decisions that affect what occurs in our world. We as humans are also believed to fit into this category (make *choices* that affect our world).[14] Consequently, for classical theists, the extent to which God can unilaterally guarantee that what occurs in this world is what he has determined should occur is primarily a function of the extent to which *God can unilaterally guarantee that humans will voluntarily (freely) do what he would have them do.*

Most classical theists agree that an action (resulting from a choice) can be considered to be voluntary (free) only if the person performing the action was not forced to do something she did not choose or prohibited from doing something she did choose.[15] In short, there is consensus that God cannot *force* another individual to act *voluntarily* "against her will."

However, the fact that God cannot force someone to act voluntarily "against her will" does not itself in any way limit God's ability to control human behavior—to ensure that we do what he would have us do—unless it is *also* the case that God cannot unilaterally control voluntary choice. Otherwise, God can always bring it about that we *voluntarily act* exactly as he would have us act simply by unilaterally ensuring that we always voluntarily make the choices he would have us make. Hence, the key question for our present purpose becomes, *Are there limitations on God's ability to unilaterally control voluntary human decision-making (and thus voluntary action)?* That is, are there limitations on God's ability to ensure that we will always make the voluntary decisions he would have us make (and thus perform the voluntary action that he would have us perform)? On this issue, as we shall see, freewill theists differ significantly with other classical theists. But in order to make the relevant distinctions, it will first be necessary to distinguish two quite different perspectives on what it means to say that a choice (decision) is voluntary.

Compatibilism Versus Incompatibilism

Compatibilists (as I will characterize them for our present purposes) are determinists with respect to human choice.[16] They maintain that given the antecedent conditions preceding a choice, no other decision is possible—that is, the person making the decision cannot chose otherwise. Furthermore, compatibilists believe that determinism is consistent with *voluntary* choice. They stipulate that a voluntary decision must be one that the person in question has herself made in the sense that there must exist an appropriate causal connection between this person's choice and the relevant cognitive and affective states—the relevant beliefs and desires—held by this person prior to the time at which the decision was made. For instance, they deny that decisions made while under the influence of drugs are necessarily voluntary, since the appropriate connection is often missing in such a case. But as long as some such link exists—as long as a decision follows from prior states of mind—compatibilists consider the choice in question voluntary, even if it is the case that the antecedent conditions allowed for no other decision.

Incompatibilists agree that a decision can be considered voluntary only if it follows in the right sort of way from beliefs and desires that the person held prior to this choice. But they are indeterminists (proponents of libertarian freedom) with respect to *voluntary* choice. That is, they believe that given the conditions preceding any voluntary decision, more than one decision must be possible—the person making the decision must be in a position to chose differently. Accordingly, they deny that determinism is compatible with voluntary choice, even in those cases where the appropriate connection exists.[17]

With this distinction in hand, we are now in a position to consider the various classical responses to the question whether God can unilaterally control voluntary human decision-making (and thus voluntary action)—the question whether he can ensure unilaterally that humans will always make the voluntary decisions he would have them make (and thus perform the voluntary action he would have them perform).

Theological Determinism

Some classical theists, often labeled *theological determinists,* believe that God can *always* ensure that humans will voluntarily make the decisions he would have them make (and thus do what he would have them do). Most theological determinists, not surprisingly, are compatibilists. While they acknowledge that given the conditions preceding any voluntary choice, only one decision is possible, it is their belief that God is able at every moment to influence a person's beliefs and desires in such a way that this person will voluntarily make the choice God would have him or her make.

These theological determinists still acknowledge, of course, that God cannot actualize a world in which a person voluntarily chooses to bring about a logically impossible state of affairs (for instance, chooses to become a married bachelor). And they readily admit that if God has decided to have a person voluntarily make a certain decision (for instance, refuse a marriage proposal), he may not be able to actualize concurrently other states of affairs that he would otherwise have been able to actualize (for instance, accepting the proposal). But in neither of these cases is the limitation related to the fact that the decisions (or subsequent actions) are voluntary. These limitations simply reflect the fact that God cannot bring about something that is logically impossible. And as already stated, classical theists do not believe that this type of "limitation" in any way hinders God from actualizing his creative goals. Accordingly, as these determinists see it, the fact that this world contains other entities who possess voluntary choice (and perform voluntary actions) places no limitation on *God's ability to control earthly affairs* (to ensure the occurrence of all that he would have come about). Or, stated differently, voluntary choice, as these theological determinists see it, is simply one of the means God can utilize to bring about that which he would have occur in our world.[18]

Surprisingly, though, some theological determinists (as I am using the term) are incompatibilists, that is, they deny that determinism is compatible with voluntary choice. Hence, they adamantly deny that a person can be considered to have chosen voluntarily if God has directly influenced her beliefs and desires in such a way that he has ensured that she will make the exact decision he would have her make. However, from the perspective of these theological determinists, this places no limitation on God's ultimate ability to ensure unilaterally that humans will always make the voluntary decisions he would have them make (and thus perform the voluntary action he would have them perform).

But how can this be? If God cannot unilaterally influence a person's decision-making process in such a way that this influence ensures (determines) that she will voluntarily make the decisions God would have her make, then how can God *ensure* that the voluntary decisions made will *always* be those that he desires? In response, these theological determinists acknowledge that God's ability to control truly voluntary incompatibilistic choice is something that "cannot possibly be reconciled before the bar of human reason."[19] In fact, it "is a mystery which we cannot expect to solve in this world."[20] But God's logic, they maintain, is above ours, and God has informed us (in Scripture) that he ultimately controls voluntary human choice. So we must simply accept that this is so. It "is the revealed antimony in terms of which we have to do our thinking."[21]

Consequently, these theological determinists agree with their compatibilistic counterparts that the existence of other entities with the capacity to choose (and thus act) voluntarily in no way limits God's ability to control earthly affairs—in no way keeps God from actualizing all of his creative goals. Again, voluntary choice (and thus action) is simply the means by which God brings about his ends. God can combine any set of self-consistent voluntary choices (and thus actions) in any compossible manner.[22] Or, to state this important point in terms of the basic question under consideration, regardless of why theological determinists believe as they do, their position on the *extent* to which God's providential power is efficacious in our world is clear: since God can unilaterally guarantee that humans will always freely choose (and thus act) as he would have them choose (and act), and humans are the only other self-determining beings, nothing can thwart God's creative power. God is never *surprised*. Nor need he ever rely on *luck* or take any *risks*. God, rather, can unilaterally guarantee that all and only that which he has determined should occur in our world will in fact come about. Freely chosen human activities simply function as desired building blocks in God's preordained creative plan.

Although freewill theists are classical theists, they reject theological determinism. However, they are not the only classical theists who do so. Freewill theists, as we will see, base their rejection of theological determinism on their indeterministic (and thus incompatibilistic) understanding of voluntary choice. But it is important to realize that some who reject theological determinism are compatibilists (believe that determinism is compatible with voluntary choice).[23]

Limited Compatibilism

As is true of all compatibilists, these *limited compatibilists*, as we shall call them, contend that for a decision to be considered voluntary, there must exist a significant causal connection between this decision and the relevant beliefs and desires held prior to the time at which the choice was made. There is, though, significant disagreement between these compatibilists and those who are theological determinists on the *exact properties* of the beliefs and desires with which a truly voluntary choice must be causally connected. Compatibilists who are theological determinists stipulate only that such causally efficacious states of mind must exist prior to the decision in question. They do not place restrictions on the manner in which these beliefs and desires are acquired or maintained. At least they do not place any restrictions on the manner in which God might bring it about that a person possesses these beliefs and desires.

For limited compatibilists, though, the situation is different. As they understand it, in order to control decisively a person's decision-making process in every context, God may need at times either to *interject new and unmotivated desires and/or beliefs* or to *eradicate certain beliefs and/or desires already present.* As they understand it, for instance, to ensure that all individuals receiving marriage proposals respond in the desired manner, God may at times need either to interject into the minds of some individuals certain beliefs and/or desires related to marriage that would not have been present otherwise or to remove certain beliefs and/or desires that would have led to the "wrong" decision. However, these compatibilists stipulate that voluntary choice must be based on "beliefs and desires . . . acquired in the right sort of way."[24] And for a person to receive new and unmotivated beliefs or desires from an external source, even a divine external source, they adamantly contend, is not to acquire these mental states in the right sort of way. John Feinberg argues, for instance, that for God to eradicate "inappropriate" beliefs and/or desires whenever necessary to ensure that "wrong" choices are never made would "obviously . . . contradict God's intention to create creatures who are compatibilistically free and get to exercise that freedom."[25]

Similarly, Martin Davies maintains that a person who receives new and unmotivated beliefs from God is like a kleptomaniac who, although aware of perfectly good reasons not to steal on certain occasions, is overcome by a sudden desire to steal and therefore does so. And a kleptomaniac, Davies points out, is "not a good example of a rational agent" (a person who has an appropriate basis for voluntary decision-making).[26] Consequently, these compatibilists conclude that God may not in every case to able to control decisively the decision-making process of individuals engaged in *voluntary* decision-making.

Moreover, limited compatibilists deny that there is any mysterious means, apart from controlling the decision-making process itself, by which God could unilaterally regulate human choice. Thus they acknowledge that to the extent God grants us voluntary choice, God may not be able to "get us to do good without constraining us"[27]—that is, may not be able to ensure unilaterally that we will always *voluntarily* make the decisions he would have us make.

This does not mean that limited compatibilists must also grant that any state of affairs actually occurring in this world is not in fact what God would have occur. It is possible, given this perspective, that the judicious use of his ability to manipulate our properly acquired beliefs and/or desires has always enabled God to order our decision-making processes in such a way that the exact decisions he would have us make have always been made voluntarily. And if this is the case, then the existence of other entities who exercise voluntary choice has not itself limited God's ability to control earthly affairs (has not kept him from bringing about all that he would have come about).

But unlike what is true within theological determinism, it may also be the case, given limited compatibilism, that God has often been unable to manipulate our decision-making processes in such a way that the exact decisions he would have had us make have in fact been made. And if this is the case, then the existence of other entities who exercise voluntary choice has in fact limited God's ability to control earthly affairs. That is, if this is the case, then it is no longer true that God's activity in this world is constrained only by his inability to bring about that which is itself self-contradictory or incompossible. Rather, the existence of other beings who exercise voluntary choice has prohibited God from bringing about self-consistent and/or compossible states of affairs that he would have brought about if it had been in his power to do so. At the very least, even if God has, up to this point, been able to actualize all and only that which is in keeping with his will, there can be no guarantee, given limited compatibilism, that this will be the case in the future. Whether God will in fact be able to control voluntary human decision-making in all cases remains an open question.

Freewill Theism

The stage is now set for a fuller discussion of freewill theism (FWT) itself. As already noted, freewill theists,[28] like both theological determinists and limited compatibilists, are classical theists in that they too maintain that God can, at least to some extent, unilaterally control earthly affairs. Like limited compatibilists, they reject the theological determinist's contention that God can unilaterally guarantee that people will always make the voluntary choices he would have them make and thus can ensure that all that occurs is in keeping with his will. But freewill theists are incompatibilists. They deny, in the words of Bruce Reichenbach, "that one agent can bring it about, either directly or indirectly by constituting the nature of the agent in a determinate manner, that another agent freely chooses or acts in a certain way."[29] Thus, unlike limited compatibilists, they deny that a person can ever be said to have chosen voluntarily if God has influenced this person's decision-making process itself in such a way that he has ensured (determined) that the choice he would have her make has in fact been made.

Freewill theists, though, sharply disagree with those incompatibilists who, as theological determinists, contend that God can still somehow bring it about that the voluntary decisions individuals make will always be the exact decisions he would have them make. As freewill theists see it, this contention is not simply an *apparent contradiction* that must nevertheless be accepted as true. They see it as an actual contradiction that must for that reason be rejected. Consequently, it should not be surprising that, unlike theological determinists and limited compatibilists, freewill theists maintain that *to the extent that God grants individuals freedom, he gives up complete control over the decisions that are made.*[30]

Moreover, freewill theists believe that God actually has granted us freedom. Specifically, they believe that God has granted us significant moral freedom of choice (action). It is *significant* in that our freedom consists of the ability to do more than simply pick among menu items or TV shows. It is extended to the most important life choices—marriage partners, schools, friends, our relationship with God. It is considered *moral* freedom in that God allows us to choose between "good" and "evil," that is, to choose between what is compatible and what is incompatible with the actualization of God's creative goals.[31]

It is possible, though, to distinguish a person's choice from the actualization of this choice, as well as to distinguish the actualization of the choice from the consequences that follow. Consider, for example, a child who is feuding with her brother at the kitchen table and is contemplating knocking over a glass of milk so that her brother's clothes will get wet. We can distinguish the choice (whether to attempt to knock over the glass) from the related action (knocking over the glass) and this action from the desired result (her brother's clothes getting wet).

Furthermore, it is clearly possible for one human to allow another to exercise choice and yet to prohibit the occurrence of the desired action and/or the anticipated consequences. It is possible, for instance, for the parent of our angry child to allow her to choose to knock over a glass of milk but to prevent her from in fact doing so by restraining her hand or by moving the glass. It is also possible for the parent to allow the glass to be knocked over but to prevent the desired results by moving the other child or by catching the spill on the table with napkins.

Accordingly, we need to consider two related questions to help clarify fully the freewill theist's position on God's ability to control earthly affairs: To what extent, if any, can God allow a person to choose freely to perform a given action but so order the circumstances that this person will, in fact, never perform the action in question? And to what extent, if any, can God allow a person to freely perform a chosen action but so order the circumstances that no undesirable consequence follows from the performance of this action?

Freewill theists do not deny that God has the capacity (power) to keep a person *in every case* from acting out her intentions and/or to prohibit undesired consequences. In every situation in which a person chooses to buy a car or eat at a given restaurant or rob a bank or abuse a child, the God of FWT possesses the power to keep the individual in question from performing the relevant actions and to keep the actions, once performed, from producing the intended results. Nor do freewill theists deny that God might in some cases be justified in intervening in this manner. Freewill theists believe that God does unilaterally control some things. Many believe, for instance, that God unilaterally created this type of world, that he may at times unilaterally intervene in our world to "keep things on track," and that he may occasionally unilaterally intervene in our personal lives (or at least in the lives of some).

Freewill theists deny, however, that God could consistently and pervasively exercise his power to intervene in this manner. For some, such divine action would be incompatible with meaningful choice. It is doubtful, they point out, that God could continually circumvent or modify our natural (psychological) laws in a pervasive, widespread manner without destroying our belief that anticipated consequences will normally follow our action—without destroying our belief in predictable regularities. But choosing to do something is inextricably tied to the concept of willing the occurrence of one state of affairs rather than another. And we cannot meaningfully will the occurrence of one state of affairs rather than another if we can have no assurance that given consequences will normally follow given actions. Thus since God desires that we exercise meaningful choice, the possibility of pervasive divine intervention, they conclude, must be ruled out.[32]

For other freewill theists, such pervasive intervention would be incompatible with God's moral character. God, they argue, has created us in such a way that we firmly believe we are free to act out our intentions within the parameters of the relevant natural (psychological) laws. In fact, much of our behavior toward others is based on the belief that we can rightfully make this assumption. Hence, since widespread intervention of the type in question would require God to deceive us in a systematic and comprehensive manner with respect to the true nature of our supposed self-determination, such intervention, they contend, is clearly behavior in which a perfectly good being would not engage.[33]

Finally, other freewill theists see continuous, widespread intervention of this sort as incompatible with God's primary creative agenda. It is true, they argue, that God has created (initiated) a world in which humans exercise libertarian freedom of choice. But this was not his primary goal. His primary goal was to create a world in which such choice would serve as the basis for voluntary human *action*, and such action can be voluntary, they maintain, only in those cases in which God does not prohibit the natural causal connections between choice and action and/or action and consequences.[34]

What is being argued here, it is important to note, is not that the God of FWT will ensure that every voluntary choice (or even most voluntary choice) is in fact actualized. A child, for instance, who freely chooses to knock over a glass of milk may in fact not be strong enough to do so or may in fact miss when attempting to hit the glass or may be stopped from doing so by an observant parent.

And God, given freewill thought, is under no obligation to ensure that this child's, or anyone else's, intended goal will in fact be realized. The contention, rather, is only that God, *as a general rule*, must allow choice to be voluntary in the sense that it is free from coercive divine manipulation.

We are now in a position to summarize the freewill response to the fundamental question of God's ability to control unilaterally earthly affairs. Since freewill theists believe that *God has chosen to create a world in which humans have been granted the power to exercise pervasive, morally significant freedom of choice (and thus action)* and that *God cannot unilaterally ensure that humans exercising free choice will make the decisions he would have them make (and thus act as he would have them act)*, freewill theists conclude that *God does not exercise unilateral control over many important aspects of what occurs in our earthly realm.*

That this is so, it must be explicitly reemphasized, is viewed as a *self-limitation.* Freewill theists acknowledge that God does not control much of what occurs. However, unlike process theists, they are adamant in their belief that this is the result of a moral choice, not an external restriction. John Hick, for instance, tells us that God could have maintained absolute control over earthly affairs but limited himself by bringing into existence free agents.[35] In similar fashion William Hasker points out that "God's capacity to control the detailed course of events is limited only by his self-restraint, not by any inability to do so."[36]

However, the fact remains that freewill theists, unlike theological determinists, must ultimately view God in a very real sense as a *risk-taker.* The God of FWT hopes that individuals will always freely choose to do what he would have them do. But for the freewill theist there can be no assurance that they will do so. Since God has chosen to grant us significant moral freedom, "the fleshing out of various details and particulars are directed and actualized by [our] choices."[37]

Conclusion

We now have a clear picture of the shared beliefs of freewill theists, beliefs that will henceforth be labeled *basic freewill theism (BFWT)*.[38] But proponents of BFWT differ on many important questions. They differ significantly, for instance, on the question of why God decided to create a world containing pervasive, significant freedom of choice, and on the question of the extent to which God can unilaterally intervene in such a world. They differ on the type of knowledge that God possesses and on the extent to which this knowledge enables him to control earthly affairs. They differ on the need for an afterlife as well as on the nature of such a realm if it exists. They differ on the approach to ethical decision-making utilized by God and how it relates to divine interventive activity.[39]

This diversity of opinion sets the stage for most of what will follow in this book. Freewill theism is a very influential theistic perspective today. I personally believe it to be at present the most popular theistic variant in both philosophical and nonphilosophical circles. But, as argued more fully in the introduction, I believe that the reality of pervasive religious diversity—the fact that seemingly sincere epistemic peers affirm differing religious perspectives—places all those interested in the "truth" of the matter under the epistemic obligation to consider seriously the explanations for reality offered by competing belief systems. Accordingly, it is vitally important, I believe, that the freewill perspective be presented as clearly as possible, and this book is my attempt at such a clarification. Specifically, what follows is primarily my attempt to determine what important *additional* beliefs, if any, about the nature of God—God's knowledge, God's moral character, the cause and purpose of evil and the efficacy of prayer—are required or prohibited by the affirmation of BFWT.[40]

2
BASIC FREEWILL THEISM & DIVINE OMNISCIENCE

PROPONENTS OF BASIC FREEWILL THEISM (BFWT) BELIEVE that God exercises some, but not total, control over earthly affairs.[1] Exactly how much control can it be held that God exercises? One key determinant, everyone agrees, is the type of knowledge that God possesses. But what type(s) of knowledge can the God of BFWT justifiably be thought to possess? And what is the exact relationship between such knowledge and God's providential activity? These are the questions that this chapter will address.

To say that God is omniscient, most philosophers and theologians agree, is to say that God knows all true propositions that are possible to know. There is, however, a great deal of disagreement about what is knowable. Those who believe that God possesses what has come to be labeled "present knowledge" (PK) maintain that God's knowledge is limited to everything that is (or has been) actual and to what follows deterministically from it. He knows, for example, exactly what Caesar was thinking when he crossed the Rubicon and how many horses he had in his army that day. He knows exactly what every politician actually feels about the policies he or she is proposing. And since God knows how the laws of nature (which he has created) function, he knows, for example, how certain weather systems will develop and what their effects will be on certain natural environments.

However, proponents of PK deny that God possesses infallible knowledge of any future state of affairs that includes free human decision-making as a causal component. God, as the ultimate psychoanalyst or behaviorist, can with great accuracy predict what individuals will freely decide to do in the future in many cases. He might well, for instance, be able to predict quite accurately who will win the American presidential election in the year 2012. However, a God with only PK cannot know infallibly who will be elected president in 2012. Given that the outcome of such choice is dependent on decisions that have yet to be made, there is nothing at present for God to know with certainty.[2]

Proponents of what is often called "simple foreknowledge" (SFK) disagree. Statements describing what will actually happen, they argue, including statements describing events related to what humans will freely do, are true now. It is true or false now that Newt Gingrich will be elected president in the year 2012 in the actual world. Not all of the relevant decisions have been made at this time. But Gingrich will either choose to run or choose not to run, he will either be nominated or not be nominated, and he will either be elected or not be elected. Thus, since God knows all true propositions, he knows now if Gingrich will be elected president in the actual world in 2012.[3]

But what about counterfactual claims? What, for example, should we say about the following statement: If Ted Kennedy had won the presidential election in 1980, he would have run again in 1984. The antecedent is false, so the statement cannot be true by virtue of the fact that it describes what actually occurred. But is it not either true or false that *if* Kennedy had won in 1980, he would have run again? Ought we not thus maintain that God knows the truth or falsity of such propositions?

Many philosophers and theologians believe that God possesses such knowledge, which is usually called "middle knowledge" (MK). They believe, that is, that God knows not only what will in fact happen in the actual world or what *could* in fact happen in all worlds, but also what *would* in fact happen in every possible situation, including what every possible free creature would do in every possible situation in which that creature could find itself.[4] They believe that God does know, for example, whether Ted Kennedy would have chosen freely to run again in 1984 if he had been elected president in 1980. As humans, we "may not know what the answer is," MK proponent Alvin Plantinga points out. But "one thing we would take for granted . . . is there is a right answer here. . . . We would reject out of hand . . . the suggestion that there simply is none."[5]

Recently some philosophers and theologians have chosen to apply the term "freewill theist" solely to those proponents of BFWT who believe that God possesses PK.[6] But is a proponent of BFWT—someone who believes that God's decision to grant us significant moral freedom limits his control of earthly affairs—actually committed to a specific model of omniscience? Or can a proponent of BFWT affirm any of the models in question?[7]

Preliminary Considerations

No one denies that PK is possible for God—that is, no one denies that it would be possible for God to know all that has occurred in the past, is occurring now and probably will occur in the future. However, many have denied that God could possess SFK or MK. Those denying the possibility of SFK normally argue that God cannot have exhaustive, infallible knowledge of future free choices, because until these choices are made, there is nothing for God to know. Those denying the possibility of MK normally argue that there are no true counterfactuals of freedom or that God's knowledge of such counterfactuals is incompatible with libertarian freedom.[8] If these critics are correct, then the primary question addressed in this chapter has been answered. The proponent of BFWT can reasonably maintain only that God possesses PK.

Is it true, though, that MK and SFK are impossible? I and many others have argued that this is not the case.[9] However, I see little value in rehearsing these technical, esoteric debates here, and am simply going to assume, therefore, that SFK and MK are possible and go on to focus my attention on the question whether the tenets of BFWT are compatible with the various models of omniscience.

Even with respect to this question, however, a well-known prima facie problem arises. Proponents of BFWT believe that for a decision to be truly voluntary, more than one choice must be possible—that is, it must be the case that the person could have chosen differently. But if God *foreknows* what we will freely do—if God has always known what our choices will be—then we cannot, it has been argued for millennia, choose differently from the way we do; thus we are not free. And if this is true, then a proponent of BFWT cannot maintain both that we exercise freedom of choice (in the libertarian sense) and that God possesses either SFK or MK (since both models presuppose foreknowledge of free choice).

But is divine foreknowledge truly incompatible with human freedom? Some philosophers affirm that it is, while at least an equal number deny that any such incompatibility exists.[10] It is my assumption that anyone reading this book will be acquainted with this issue, and I have nothing new to add. (In fact, I am not certain that there is anything new to be added.) Hence, in order to allow us to consider some important issues on which there does remain much to be said, I am also going to assume that there is no necessary incompatibility between divine foreknowledge and human freedom.

Basic Freewill Theism and Middle Knowledge

A number of philosophers have recently argued that, even if the concept of MK is itself coherent, the amount of power (and thus control) that MK affords God is incompatible with BFWT. Some claim (or at least imply), contrary to the fundamental tenets of BFWT, that MK furnishes God with sufficient power to bring about *exactly* what he desires in a world containing individuals with libertarian freedom, and that he can do so without significant intervention. William Craig has argued, for instance, that "since [a God with MK] knows what any free creature would do in any situation, he can, by creating the appropriate situations, bring it about that creatures will achieve his ends and purposes and that they will do so *freely*. . . . In his infinite intelligence, God is able to plan a world in which his designs are achieved by creatures acting freely."[11]

A specific illustration may help clarify what Craig seems to have in mind. Let us suppose that I want my six-year-old son, Andrew, to read ten pages of Dr. Seuss's classic *Green Eggs and Ham* before bed tonight. If I possess the power of the God of theological determinism, I can ensure that he will decide freely to read the pages in question either by irresistibly influencing his compatibilistically free will or in some mysterious way unilaterally bringing it about that he will freely desire—in a libertarian sense—to read the pages I want him to read.

The situation is quite different if I cannot unilaterally control human freedom and possess only PK (which entails that I do not have infallible knowledge of how individuals will use their freedom in the future). In this case, to the extent that I allow Andrew to choose freely what to read, I cannot guarantee that he will read the pages that I want him to read. I can, of course, still *make* him read the ten pages, but then he will not be doing so freely. I cannot have it both ways.

If I possess MK, however, then I am again in a much stronger position. I still cannot unilaterally compel Andrew to decide freely to do what I want him to do in any situation. But I do know how he will respond freely in every possible situation in which I could request (in a noncoercive manner) that he read the ten pages I have in mind. I know, for example, how he would respond if I asked him in a soft voice right after dinner, how he would respond if I waited until right before he went to bed, how he would respond if I told him that his teacher wanted him to read these pages, and so on.

Now let us suppose that I "see" with my MK that Andrew will freely choose to read the desired pages if I ask him to do so in a soft voice right before bed. In this case I again possess the power to control what Andrew freely reads. By asking him in a soft voice right before bed to read the desired pages, I can bring it about that he will do exactly what I want, even though he will still be acting freely in a libertarian sense.

As Craig sees it, a God with MK can employ this same technique to bring about exactly what he wants in all cases. God cannot force us to desire freely to do exactly what he wants in any situation. But since God knows what we will freely decide to do in every possible set of circumstances, God can simply bring about those circumstances (that situation) in which he knows we will freely decide to do exactly what he wants done. In this way he can "plan a world in which his designs are achieved by creatures acting freely." Craig grants that this is a very complex undertaking for God, given all the free choices involved. In his mind, however, this only makes God more awe-inspiring.[12]

In response to Craig, it must first be acknowledged (again) that a God with MK has the potential for more control over earthly affairs than does a God with only PK or SFK. A being who knows ahead of time exactly how things will turn out, given all the available options, does, in principle, have a decided advantage over a being who does not have this type of comparative foreknowledge. But is it true that a God with MK—like the God of the theological determinist—can *always* bring it about that we "will achieve his ends and purposes and that [we] will do so freely?"

In one sense the answer is clearly no. Let us revisit the scenario with my son. If I am fortunate enough to "see" with my MK that there does exist a situation I can bring about in which he will freely choose to read exactly what I want read, then I can bring it about that he "will achieve [my] ends and purposes and that [he] will do so freely." But does such a situation actually exist? Will there exist an actualizable situation in which Andrew freely reads what I would have him read?

Craig's comments imply that the answer is yes. But this is incorrect. Since we are assuming that Andrew possesses libertarian freedom in every one of the different situations (differing sets of circumstances) in which his choice to read can be made, it is possible that he will choose freely *not* to read the pages in question in even one of these situations. That is, there may be no actualizable situation in which he freely reads the pages in question. And if this is the case, then even though I still retain my power to "see" what he will freely decide to do in every context, I no longer possess the power to bring it about that he will read the pages in question freely. I must either take away his freedom or settle for something less than I had originally wanted.

The same is true for each of us in relation to a God who possesses MK. It seems reasonable to assume that by "creating the appropriate situation" God with MK could at times bring it about that what we freely decide to do is what "will achieve his ends and purposes." It is possible that he could often (even always) do so. However, with respect to some (or even many) of these ends and purposes, there may be no such "appropriate situation" for God to create.

Consider again, for instance, the next presidential election. It may be that by creating certain situations, God will be able to bring it about that I will decide freely to vote exactly as God desires that I vote. However, since I will possess libertarian freedom in every situation in which I vote freely, it is possible that I will decide freely in every such situation not to vote as God would have me vote. That is, it may be that there exists no "appropriate situation" in which I freely decide to vote as God desires me to vote. And if this is so, then God will in this case either have to take away my freedom and make me vote the way he wants or have to settle for something less than the ideal.

To state this important point in yet another way, a God with MK might be quite lucky. With respect to all or most of his "ends and purposes," God might be able to "see" that there are actualizable situations in which individuals freely choose to do what he desires. But then again, he might be quite unlucky. God might "see" with respect to many or most of his "ends and purposes" that there are few, if any, actualizable situations in which individuals freely choose to do what God wants to be done.

Thus it is quite misleading to assert that a God with MK can "plan" the world he wants in the sense that he can, "by creating the appropriate situations, bring it about that creatures will achieve his ends and purposes and that they will do so freely." This certainly is the case for the God of theological determinism. This God, as we have seen, can use free choices as "building blocks" in designing the world of his choice. However, since a God with MK cannot control what we will choose to do in any situation in which we possess meaningful freedom, it can hardly be said that MK allows God to "plan" the world God wants in the sense that he can ensure that the most desirable "ends and purposes" of which he can conceive will always be achieved. Rather, it is possible for a God with MK to be disappointed in the sense that he may often have to settle for much less than the ideal.[13]

What this means, for our purposes, is that there exists no inherent incompatibility between the concept of MK and the concept of self-limited divine sovereignty affirmed by proponents of BFWT. A God who possesses MK is clearly in a position to exercise more control over earthly affairs than one who does not. But MK does not ensure that God can achieve all desired ends. Thus the belief that God possesses MK is not incompatible with the belief that God's decision to grant individuals freedom of choice limits his control over earthly affairs.

But is it not at least true, as William Hasker argues, that a God with MK, like the God of theological determinism, takes *no* risks?

> Short of absolute predestination, the only theory known to me that eliminates risk taking on God's part is the theory of middle knowledge. For on this theory God's knowledge of the future is *not* derived from the actual occurrence of the future events, but rather from the knowledge of the counterfactuals of freedom together with God's knowledge concerning which states of affairs he will actualize. But the knowledge of the counterfactuals is prior, in the order of explanation, to God's decisions about what to create, so that these decisions are indeed informed by full and complete knowledge of the respective outcomes of any possible choice God might make. The element of risk is eliminated entirely.[14]

Thus since the God of BFWT (as noted in chapter one) is a risk-taker, must we not conclude that MK is incompatible with BFWT?

In one sense Hasker's contention that MK eliminates risk is correct. A God with MK, unlike the God of theological determinism, must rely on luck, may experience the divine equivalent of disappointment and may need to intervene significantly in earthly affairs. However, like the God of theological determinism, a God with MK knows exactly what will happen (including how he will react to a given state of affairs) before he begins to actualize any creative option. Thus creation is in one sense not a gamble or risk in any way.

In a more important sense, however, Hasker's contention that MK eliminates risk is based on a confusion. Specifically, Hasker is confusing two distinct understandings of what it means for God to be a risk-taker: God is a risk-taker in the sense that he commits himself to a course of action without full knowledge of the outcome; and God is a risk-taker in the sense that he adopts certain overall strategies—for example, the granting of significant freedom—which create the potential for the occurrence of events that he wishes would not occur.

It has already been acknowledged that a God with MK is not a risk-taker in the first sense. He knows exactly what will happen in the world he is actualizing. But the relationship between a God with MK and risk-taking in the second sense, as we shall see, is much more complex. A God with MK, it must be acknowledged, is not *required* to be a risk-taker in the second sense (not required to create the potential for undesired occurrences). Such a God could decide *not* to actualize a world in which individuals possess significant freedom, thus exercising total control over earthly affairs.

However, if a God with MK does decide to actualize a world containing individuals with significant freedom, the situation is quite different. There will be many possible worlds containing free creatures who do exactly what God would have them do. But as we have seen, if God has MK, he is not able to *ensure* that a possible world in which all inhabitants freely do exactly what he wants is among the actualizable options. Hence, if we assume that God has MK and has decided to create a world containing free creatures—which is exactly what proponents of MK do in fact maintain—then God is a risk-taker in the second sense. This type of risk, moreover, is exactly the type of risk to which the proponent of BFWT believes God has exposed himself by granting humans significant freedom. Consequently, any alleged incompatibility between MK and BFWT that is based on the risk inherent in BFWT can be disregarded.[15]

Basic Freewill Theism and Present Knowledge

No philosopher argues directly that a proponent of BFWT cannot justifiably maintain that God possesses only PK. However, one philosopher, Francis Beckwith, has recently argued that no Christian who holds a high view of Scripture (who believes the Bible to be an authoritative communication from God) can affirm PK alone.[16] Thus since many freewill theists (in fact some of its leading proponents) are Christians and do in fact believe Scripture to be authoritative, I believe it worthwhile to analyze Beckwith's claim.

Beckwith bases his argument on the test for a true prophet found in Deuteronomy 18:22 (JB): "When a prophet speaks in the name of Yahweh and the thing does not happen and the word is not fulfilled, then it has not been said by Yahweh. The prophet has spoken presumptuously. You have nothing to fear from him." Taken at face value, Beckwith explains, this passage clearly indicates that

(1) when a person is predicting the future *as a spokesperson for God,* he or she cannot be inaccurate; there can be no possible world in which a person can be speaking *for God* and be wrong.

However, to deny that God has exhaustive knowledge of the future, he argues, is to acknowledge that

(2) "it is within the realm of possibility that God could make a mistake about the future,"

which is, he believes, simply another way of saying that

(3) "in some possible world God makes a mistake in predicting the future."[17]

Accordingly, since (3) is clearly incompatible with (1), no Christian with a high view of Scripture, Beckwith concludes, can affirm PK.

In response, it must first be noted that those who affirm PK need not necessarily deny (1). They can, in a certain sense, accept that there is no possible world in which a spokesperson for God could ever be wrong.[18] Moreover, proponents of PK need not deny (2). They need not deny that God *could* in some possible world make inaccurate predictions about the future, if this is interpreted as a statement about God's capacity or power to act. In fact, they can acknowledge that in *any* possible world in which creatures possess true freedom of choice, God possesses the capacity to utter inaccurate predictions (for instance, by predicting on the basis of that which he does not yet know with certainty).

However, (3)—the claim that there is some possible world in which God does in fact utter mistaken predictions—is *not* equivalent to (2)—the contention that there are possible worlds in which God could (in the sense of having the capacity to) do so. Just as it does not follow from the fact that God has the capacity to treat individuals unfairly that he ever actually does so (or even that there is any possible world in which he would do so), it does not follow from the fact that God has the capacity to utter inaccurate predictions in every possible world containing free creatures that he actually does so in any such world. (3) follows from (2) only if we also assume that God has in fact had his spokespersons utter a prophecy (a prediction about the future) based on data to which he did not have complete access. However, this is something that those who are proponents of PK do deny. In fact, they deny that there is any possible world containing free creatures in which he does so. Thus they reject (3).

Consequently, proponents of PK remain free to affirm (1), that is, remain free to acknowledge that a true spokesperson for God will never make a prediction about the future that even could be wrong, while justifiably maintaining that God does not have total knowledge of all future states of affairs. Is it not the case, though, that the Bible contains unconditional, infallible predictions about the future that *require that God have infallible knowledge of future free choices?* Was it not infallibly predicted, for example, that those whom Jesus came to save would freely reject him (1 Pet 1)?

Proponents of PK do not deny that some prophetic utterances, *when considered in isolation from the overall teaching of Scripture*, can appear to presuppose infallible divine knowledge of future free choices. But they deny that any such utterance requires that God have such knowledge. They maintain, rather, that all prophetic utterances can be interpreted as one of the following: an announcement ahead of time that what God intends to ensure will occur, conditional prophecies that leave the outcome open or predictions based on God's exhaustive knowledge of the past and present. Not surprisingly, critics of PK often find such interpretations strained and unconvincing. But this is in an important sense irrelevant. If there is one hermeneutical issue on which most conservative Christians agree, it is that the interpretation of any given verse (or passage) must ultimately be determined by the overall teaching of Scripture on the issue at hand. Accordingly, since few claim that the interpretations of problem passages offered by proponents of PK are logically impossible, the real issue is what Scripture as a whole teaches concerning the scope of God's knowledge.

Those who affirm PK do not deny that there are some verses (in addition to those related to prophecy) that seem at face value to support the idea that God has exhaustive knowledge of the future. In Isaiah 46:9-10, for instance, we read, "I am God, and there is none like me. I make known the end from the beginning." However, proponents of PK maintain that when we consider Scripture as a whole, what we find emerging is not the picture of a God who is working out some prefect, preordained plan that was decided upon long before creation. What emerges, rather, is a portrait of a God who not only interacts with his creation, responding to what he experiences in an attempt to bring about his desired goals, and who "changes his mind," modifying plans (or at least the means by which he intends to accomplish his plans) on the basis of information he did not possess at the time that his plans were originally formulated, but a God who is pleased with us when we act according to his hopes, or disappointed with us when we do not act as he had hoped we would act.

Critics of PK are quick to interpret all such passages as anthropomorphisms (the attribution of human form to God), anthropopathisms (the attribution of human feelings to God) or some other figure of speech. But the question at hand is not whether the critic can coherently maintain that God has exhaustive knowledge of the future. The question is whether the proponent of PK can deny that this is so. Accordingly, critics of PK must in this context do more than simply point out problem passages—that is, passages that appear to them to portray God as one who possesses exhaustive knowledge of the future—and then complain that they find the responses of proponents of PK to these passages to be unconvincing or ad hoc.

To challenge successfully the right of a Christian with a high view of Scripture to affirm PK, what critics must argue is that it is *impossible*, given neutral hermeneutical principles, to deny that specific passages require that God possess exhaustive knowledge and/or to deny that Scripture *as a whole* portrays God as one who possesses such knowledge. I do not believe, however, that any such argument has yet been produced. (Nor do I believe that such an argument will or even can be produced.) Thus as I see it, proponents of PK retain the right to offer their perspective as a viable alternative for consideration by any sincere Christian.[19]

Moreover, I cannot myself conceive of any other basis for arguing that FWT is incompatible with MK, SFK and/or PK. Accordingly, it is my contention that a freewill theist can justifiably affirm any of these three models of omniscience.

Simple Foreknowledge and Providential Control

Since we will be discussing the practical significance of these differing models of omniscience in forthcoming chapters, it is important to clarify one final issue. As has been mentioned repeatedly, a God who possesses MK is in a position to exercise more control over earthly affairs than a God who possesses only SFK or PK. However, what is the comparative status of SFK and PK in this regard? A God with SFK knows more than a God with PK alone. But is a God with SFK in a position to exercise more providential control over earthly affairs than is a God with PK alone? On the surface it might appear that the answer is obviously yes. After all, it might be argued, just as a person who foreknew next week's winning number would be in a much better position to win the lottery than would someone without such knowledge, so too would a God who foreknew what was to occur in the future be in a better position to ensure his desired ends. In this case, however, appearances are deceptive. To help illustrate why this is so, let us consider two hypothetical situations in which a God having SFK might appear to have providential advantage over a God having PK alone.

Case 1. Tom has asked Sue to marry him, and she has prayed over his proposal. Among the beliefs that God holds as he considers Sue's prayer is the belief that Sue will respond negatively if her spouse dies a tragic death soon after marriage, and thus that she ought not be encouraged to marry if it is known or believed that such a death will occur. Accordingly, because (and only because) he *foresees* that Tom is going to die in a horrible automobile accident a year from now, God attempts to influence Sue not to accept the proposal.

Case 2. God wishes that the lost ark of the covenant not be found again until the Second Coming. *Foreseeing* that no one will ever look inside a particular cave not far from Jerusalem, God contrives to have the ark slip from its litter and tumble into that very cave.[20]

What makes these two cases so persuasive initially is that if God could utilize the foreknowledge in question, his ability to bring about his desired ends would be greatly enhanced. If a God with

SFK could utilize foreknowledge of what will happen to Tom in deciding how to respond to Sue's requests for guidance, God's ability to offer sound advice clearly would be increased. And if a God with SFK were able to utilize his foreknowledge to identify actualizable conditions under which he could ensure (or even improve the chances) that the ark would not be discovered until the Second Coming, then again the providential value of such knowledge would be beyond question.

However, in neither of these cases can a God with SFK actually utilize his foreknowledge in the sense required for such knowledge to be providentially beneficial. To help illustrate why this is so, let us return first to the case of our prescient lottery player. Our player can beneficially utilize her foreknowledge of the winning numbers only if she has access to this information before she decides what numbers she will play. However, if our player has always possessed complete foreknowledge, then there has never been a time when she foreknew what the winning numbers would be but did not already know *at this same time* what numbers she would choose to play. Thus if our player has complete foreknowledge, her knowledge of next week's winning numbers cannot influence what numbers she chooses to play and is of no practical benefit.

Not surprisingly, the same basic problem arises in both of the examples that allege providentially beneficial divine foreknowledge. God's foreknowledge of Tom's death can be utilized by God in the providentially beneficial manner being presupposed only if this information influences how he responds to Sue. And this can occur only if God has access to this information before he makes the decision in question. But if God has complete foreknowledge, then there can never be a time when God foreknows that Tom will die but does not at this same time also foreknow how he will respond to Sue's request. That is, there can never be a time when God foreknows what will happen to Tom but does not already know how he will respond to Sue. Consequently, if God has complete foreknowledge, then foreknowledge of Tom's death becomes providentially irrelevant.

Likewise, if God has complete foreknowledge in our second case, then there is no time when God knows that no one will ever look inside a particular cave but does not already know also whether he will (or will not) in fact contrive to have the ark fall into this cave. Hence God's exhaustive prehension of the cave's history cannot be considered providentially relevant to the decision in question.

Moreover, it seems to me that we would be forced to reach the same conclusion in any other test case we might consider. Since there can never be a time when a God who possesses complete SFK does not know all that will occur, and since foreknowledge can be utilized in a providentially beneficial manner only if there is a time at which what is foreknown can influence a divine decision that is itself not also already foreknown, there can exist no conceivable context in which SFK would enable God to make providentially beneficial decisions that he would not be able to make without this knowledge.[21] At least this will be my assumption through the remainder of the book.[22]

Conclusion

We have seen that no necessary connection exists between BFWT and any specific model of divine omnipotence. I personally believe that God possesses only PK.[23] However, as I see it, there is nothing inherent in BFWT itself that precludes other freewill theists from justifiably affirming either SFK or MK.

3
BASIC FREEWILL THEISM & GOD'S MORAL NATURE (GOODNESS)

S O FAR WE HAVE BEEN CONCERNED PRIMARILY WITH GOD'S POW-
er, specifically, the extent to which the God of BFWT—a God
who cannot unilaterally control voluntary choice—can exercise
providential control over earthly affairs. But the extent to which
God's power can guarantee his desired ends is not the only issue
of significance when considering the relationship that exists
between the God of BFWT and the world. God's moral nature
is also at issue. Upon what basis does God, as a perfectly good
being, determine what he would have come about in our world?
That is, what moral principles serve as the basis for divine
decision-making as God identifies that which he desires to
accomplish? The purpose of this chapter is to consider various
perspectives on this question and to determine which, if any, the
proponent of BFWT—hereafter identified simply as a freewill
theist—can or must affirm.

Just as there is no uniform response among theists to the question of what it means for God to be omnipotent, so there is no

uniform response to the question of what it means for God to be perfectly good. For most, it has meant at the very least that God is morally praiseworthy in every case—that there is no context in which God's actions and attitudes are deserving of anything less than the highest moral praise.[1] But what exactly is it about God's actions and attitudes that make them worthy of such praise? For many, it is at least the fact that God always does what ought to be done. In the words of Thomas Morris, God "never acts in a way contrary to true moral principles."[2] But what are these moral principles that guide divine decision-making as God determines what he would have come about in our world?

Guiding Principles

Although many principles have been suggested, most fall into two basic categories: those that govern God's relationship with our world as a whole and those that govern his relationship with specific components within our world, for example, the natural environment, the lower animals and humans. With respect to our world as a whole, many theists, including many freewill theists, have traditionally maintained that God, as a perfectly good being, is obligated to maximize value (goodness, perfection). There has not always been agreement on what God considers to be of greatest value. Suggestions include God's glory and the spiritual and/or social well-being of his sentient creations. But many have maintained in true Leibnizian fashion that if God is perfectly good, the following principle guides his activity:

(P1) A necessary condition for the actualization of any possible world is that this world, as a whole, be the best actualizable option, that is, the option with maximal net value.[3]

Recently, though, it has become fashionable to argue that there can be no maximally valuable (best actualizable) creative option for God and therefore that (P1) cannot be considered a possible creative obligation. What is often maintained instead is that God's creative activity is governed by one of the following principles:

(P2) A necessary condition for the actualization of any possible world is that this world, as a whole, be one of tremendous value—that is, be a world with a very large net positive balance of value; or,

(P3) A necessary condition for the actualization of any possible world is that this world, as a whole, be good—that is, have a net positive balance of value.[4]

To which, if any, of these three principles is the freewill theist committed? Let us first consider (P1)—the contention that a perfectly good God must actualize that actualizable world with the highest net positive value. If it is true that there can be no maximally valuable creative option for God, then of course no theist, including no freewill theist, can maintain that (P1) outlines a moral obligation that God must fulfill. But is it true that there can be no maximally valuable creative option for God?

The arguments to this end take many specific forms, but all incorporate some version of the following general line of reasoning:

(1) The set of actualizable worlds containing differing degrees of value (goodness, perfection) is infinite.

(2) An infinite set of actualizable worlds cannot contain a world with a maximal or optimum degree of value.

(3) God cannot create that which does not exist.

(4) Thus God cannot create the (or a) maximally valuable actualizable world.[5]

This argument is valid. However, as I have argued in a previous essay, it may not be sound.[6] For most theists to claim that God is omniscient is to claim at the very least that his knowledge is eternal and exhaustive, that is, that God has always known all true propositions.

However, for each actualizable world (W), "W is an actualizable world" and "P is the net amount of value (perfection, goodness) in W″ are true propositions.[7] Accordingly, if God is essentially omniscient, then it would appear that he has always possessed not only knowledge of all actualizable worlds, but also specific, total knowledge of the net amount of value in each, even if the set of such worlds is infinite.[8] And *if* God knows the amount of value in each actualizable world, it may be that he can conceive of these worlds in some order of intrinsic worth and thus identify a best actualizable world (or best set of actualizable worlds).

The claim that God could possess specific, total knowledge of the net amount of value in an infinite set of actualizable worlds is, I readily grant, quite controversial. However, I am not convinced that this contention cannot be affirmed rationally, and consequently I am not convinced that (P1) must be rejected, that is, that all must agree that God cannot have knowledge of a best actualizable world.

But even if I am right, (P1) remains problematic for some theists. God can satisfy (P1)—that is, can ensure that he has actualized that actualizable world with the highest net positive value—only if he could assess the overall value of all actualizable worlds in their entirety *before creation*. However, if God does not possess middle knowledge (MK), that is, if God does not know what would happen given any possible scenario, then God did not know before creation how much value would actually accrue in any world he might initiate. Hence for those theists (including those freewill theists) who deny that God possesses MK, (P1) does not stipulate a possible obligation (a task that can be performed) even if there could be a maximally valuable actualizable world.

However, what if we assume that God does possess MK, and thus that (P1) does describe a task that is possible for God to perform? Is (P1) a divine obligation that a *freewill theist* who grants God MK can or must affirm?

Clearly there are interpretations of "maximal value" that render (P1) incompatible with BFWT. For example, a freewill theist could not affirm (P1) if it were claimed that a world can be maximally valuable only if human freedom is never allowed to thwart God's will in that world. Furthermore, as we shall see, many theists (including most freewill theists) believe that a perfectly good God must act in certain ways regardless of the overall consequences (is subject to deontological obligations). And a theist of this sort cannot affirm (P1) if "maximal value" is interpreted in a strictly consequential sense—that is, if the affirmation of (P1) commits God in some a priori fashion to the actualization (or attempted actualization) of the highest net value, regardless of the means by which this is accomplished.

However, if a freewill theist who affirms MK is allowed to interpret "maximal value" as desired (i.e., is allowed to interpret "maximal value" in a way compatible with BFWT in general and any additional moral obligations determined to apply to God), there then appears to be no reason why she *cannot* affirm (P1). I find nothing inherent in BFWT, though, that requires that a freewill theist do so.

But what if there is no maximally valuable world? That is, what if (P1) does not describe a possible divine task? Can, or must, a freewill theist then affirm either (P2) or (P3)—maintain that God is obligated to create a world that has tremendous value or at least a positive balance of value? Neither (P2) nor (P3) stipulates an impossible task for a God with MK. And unlike (P1), neither *necessarily* describes a task (obligation) that is impossible for a God even without MK. It is true that if God does not have MK, he cannot know at the time he initiates a given world containing free creatures exactly how much positive or negative value will accrue apart from divine intervention. But he could still in principle commit himself before creation to as much unilateral intervention as necessary to ensure that this world will have some (or much) net positive value, and in this way satisfy (P2) or (P3).

Unfortunately, when we focus our discussion on the God of

BFWT, things become more complex. Freewill theists do not deny that God can (and does) at times unilaterally override human freedom for some good end. But they believe that God is committed to the actualization of an earthly realm in which a significant number of individuals exercise significant freedom a significant amount of the time. Moreover, they deny that God can unilaterally control the decision-making of free creatures. Accordingly, unless freewill theists who deny that God possesses MK also assume that the positive value generated by the reality of significant freedom alone and/or the existence of some blissful nonearthly realm will outweigh whatever negative value the exercise of this earthly freedom might produce, they cannot maintain that God is in a position to ensure that any world he initiates will in fact be a world with even net positive value—that is, they cannot maintain that even (P2) or (P3) describes a possible task for God. They can reasonably maintain only that God is obligated to *attempt* in every way possible to initiate a world possessing the relevant property found in (P2) or (P3). In other words, without making the assumptions in question, a freewill theist who denies that God possesses MK can coherently affirm only that God, as a perfectly good being, is under one of the following obligations:

(P2*) God must always attempt to produce a world with tremendous net positive value;

or,

(P3*) God must always attempt to produce a world with a positive net balance of value.

I see no reason, though, why a freewill theist cannot assume that the positive value generated by the reality of significant freedom alone and/or the existence of some blissful nonearthly realm outweighs whatever negative value the exercise of this earthly freedom might produce. Thus I see no reason why a freewill theist cannot *choose* to affirm either (P2) or (P3). And I certainly see no reason why a freewill theist cannot *choose* to affirm at least (P2*) or (P3*).

The question whether any of these principles must be affirmed is slightly more difficult. As I see it, there is nothing inherent in BFWT that requires a proponent to maintain that God must produce (or must attempt to produce) a world with tremendous value—that is, that God must affirm either (P2) or (P2*). In fact, I do not believe there is anything inherent in BFWT that *requires* a proponent to maintain even that a perfectly good God must produce (or must attempt to produce) a world with a positive net balance of value—that requires the affirmation of either (P3) or (P3*).

To my knowledge, though, there is no freewill theist who does not believe that God is obligated, at the very least, to create (or to attempt to create) a world with positive net value. (Nor can I conceive of any reason why a freewill theist would want to think otherwise.) Consequently, while it is not quite correct to maintain that freewill theists must affirm even (P3) or (P3*), it can be said that freewill theists *do* in fact consider God, at the very least, to act in accordance with one of these obligations.

As noted earlier, however, most theists, when considering the moral principles that guide God's behavior, do not limit themselves to considering only those principles that govern God's relationship with our world as a whole. They also identify principles that govern his relationship with specific components within our world. Some of these principles stipulate divine intentions with respect to the natural realm. Many theists believe, for instance, that God has promised to sustain the natural order for as long as there is sentient life on earth. Other principles describe God's attitude toward animals in general. Most theists maintain, for instance, that a perfectly good God will never be indifferent to the present state of any living thing.

However, the most important of these relational principles for our purposes are the ones that stipulate the required relationship between a perfectly good creator and his human creations. Some of these "obligations" are quite general and are not very controversial. Almost all theists maintain, for example, that God will forgive those who contritely confess their wrongdoing. We live, though, in a world in which many innocent individuals suffer tremendously. And this suffering is seen by many as incompatible with the existence of a perfectly good God. Hence the question whether a perfectly good God is obligated to shield us from or recompense us for undeserved pain and suffering continues to be as important as it is controversial.

Divine Obligations

Many "moral obligations" (moral principles) of this type have been suggested, but I will discuss the four that I believe are most relevant:

(M1) A necessary condition for the actualization of any possible world containing sentient, self-determining beings is that God not allow any such being to suffer evil that God could prevent without negatively impacting his creative goals.

(M2) A necessary condition for the actualization of any possible world containing sentient, self-determining beings is that this world not contain even one instance of unrecompensed suffering by an innocent being of this type, even if such suffering is a necessary means to accomplish a very good end within this world.

(M3) A necessary condition for the actualization of any possible world containing sentient, self-determining beings is that this world not contain any such being whose life, through no fault of its own, is not on balance worth living, even if each instance of suffering encountered by this being is a necessary condition for some very good end within this world.

(M4) A necessary condition for the actualization of any possible world containing sentient, self-determining beings is that God do everything possible within the legitimate constraints inherent in this world to maximize the quality of life for such beings.[9]

(M1) is obviously the most minimal of these moral obligations. It allows God to cause or to permit evil in our lives as long as this evil serves any divine purpose—builds character, punishes wrongdoing, brings glory to God, et cetera. It does not require that God in any way recompense us for the evil we experience, even if we are completely innocent. In fact, (M1) is compatible with the Calvinistic contention that God at times directly inflicts unrecompensed suffering on one person solely or primarily for the sake of another. However, this principle does stipulate that a perfectly good God will never cause or allow any person to experience evil out of caprice or out of a lack of concern. Given (M1), a perfectly good God will allow us to experience only evil that is an unavoidable byproduct of, or a necessary condition for, the actualization of something that God wishes to accomplish in our world.[10]

I am not certain that a freewill theist must affirm (M1). That is, I do not find anything inherent in classical theism in general (or in BFWT in particular) that renders the denial of (M1) impossible. On the other hand, I am not aware of any freewill theist (or classical theist) who *does not* at least affirm (M1). And I see no reason why this should not be so, since (M1) appears to outline the very minimum of what can be required of a perfectly good being.

On the other end of the spectrum are (M2) and (M3), which require a great deal of God. (M2), the more stringent of the two obligations, is perhaps most poignantly stated in the rhetorical question posed by Dostoyevsky's Ivan in *The Brothers Karamazov*:

Imagine that it is you yourself who are erecting the edifice of human destiny with the aim of making men happy in the end, giving them peace and contentment at last, but that to do that it is absolutely necessary, and indeed quite inevitable, to torture to death only one tiny creature, . . . would you consent to be the architect on those conditions?[11]

(M3) is slightly less demanding. It does not require a perfectly good God to refrain from actualizing a world that contains any unrecompensed suffering. But it does obligate God to create a world in which we as humans have lives that are on balance worth living.[12]

An assessment of the relationship between these two principles and BFWT initially raises the same problem encountered with respect to (P1). Since a God with MK knows before creation the total history of all actualizable worlds, including the total life history of every individual within any such world, (M2) and (M3) clearly outline possible tasks for such a being. A God with MK could choose not to create any world in which an innocent person would suffer unrecompensed evil or someone's life would not on the whole be worth living.

However, if God does not possess MK, then he did not know before creation with certainty the life history of any individual who would be allowed to exercise free choice. Thus a God without MK can create in accordance with (M2) or (M3) only if he commits himself to as much unilateral intervention as necessary to ensure that no innocent suffering goes unrecompensed or that no innocent individual's life is not on balance worth living. But since the God of BFWT is committed to the actualization of an earthly realm in which a significant number of individuals exercise significant freedom a significant amount of the time and cannot unilaterally control the decision-making of free creatures, the God of BFWT who does not possess MK cannot *ensure* that the conditions stipulated in (M2) or (M3) will be met in *this earthly realm*. Thus it is only if a freewill theist who assumes that God does not possess MK also assumes that all innocent individuals will eventually exist in a nonearthly realm in which "the scales are balanced" that (M2) or (M3) can be affirmed. Otherwise, it can be held only that God is obligated to attempt in every way possible to initiate a world with the relevant property found in (M2) or (M3). That is, it can be maintained only that God is obligated to act in accordance with one of the following variations of (M2) or (M3):

(M2*) God must always attempt to recompense innocent suffering to whatever extent possible.

(M3*) God must attempt to ensure that every person has a life that is on the whole worth living.

Although (M2) and (M3) contain very demanding requirements, I see nothing that prohibits a freewill theist from affirming either of these proposed principles, even if she denies that God possesses MK and thus must also affirm the existence of a nonearthly realm in which all will be made right. On the other hand, I find nothing in the tenets of theism in general (or of BFWT in particular) that would require a freewill theist to affirm either—to maintain that God must in fact recompense all innocent suffering or ensure that life is worth living for all.

But ought not freewill theists at least affirm (M2*) and/or (M3*)? That is, ought not freewill theists maintain that God is at the very least obligated to do what he can to compensate innocent suffering and/or make life on balance worth living, even if they deny that God, as a perfectly good being, must always be successful? This is an important question. However, since (M2*) and (M3*) are weaker obligations than the task stipulated in (M4) (the contention that God is obligated to do all within his power to maximize the quality of life for each individual in our world), I will withhold further comment on (M2*) and (M3*) until discussion of (M4) has been completed.

The "Quality of Life" Controversy

Since many, if not most, versions of the problem of evil are based on the contention that a perfectly good God would do more to rid our world of pain and suffering, all parties agree that (M4) is a very important principle, perhaps the most important principle of its type.[13] So it is crucial to determine the exact relationship between BFWT and this alleged divine obligation.

What is first important to note is that (M4) is not subject to the type of MK difficulty inherent in some of the other principles. What is stipulated is only that God must do all that he can within the legitimate constraints inherent in a world. And among those constraints in any world in which God does not possess MK is the fact that God can never be sure of having done all that in fact could have been done. So what follows (if God does not possess MK) is not that (M4) is impossible, but only that God is obligated to *attempt* to maximize the quality of life for all.

It might be argued, however, that (M4), like (P1), stipulates an impossible task for God. Just as there can be no "best" actualizable world, someone might maintain, there can be no maximal state of existence for any given individual, since for every state of existence we might identify as such, there would, in principle, always be another state of existence with even higher quality that God could (or could attempt to) produce.

Such reasoning, though, would be misguided in this context. Even if we cannot coherently conceive of one specific state of existence that represents the highest quality of life possible for an individual, we can coherently conceive of an *ideal* state of human existence—a state of existence in which an individual possesses all and only those properties that we believe make life worth living. (We can coherently conceive, for instance, of a state of existence in which an individual experiences no gratuitous evil, lives in a harmonious relationship with her "natural" environment, feels fulfilled as a being, and possesses good health. And many would plausibly consider such a state ideal.)

Accordingly, even if it is not possible to maintain coherently that God is obligated to do what he can to ensure that each individual will experience a maximal state of existence, it is possible to maintain meaningfully that God is obligated to attempt to make each person's life as ideal as possible (regardless of the manner in which "ideal" is defined). Furthermore, not only is this interpretation of (M4) perfectly reasonable, it best captures what those concerned with the "maximization" of human existence normally have in mind. Consider, for example, the common atheistic contention that a caring God would do more to make our lives worth living. Those making this claim are not troubled because they believe that the actual world is not the *most* satisfying or pleasing state in which humans could exist. They are troubled because they believe that the actual world is a world that does not reflect all that an omnibenevolent Creator would have chosen to do for his created beings. That is, such individuals are troubled because they assume that an omnibenevolent God would create a world in which God does everything possible to ensure that the beings therein possess some basic set of ideal properties. But they see little evidence that this obligation has been met in our world.

Or let us consider the common conservative Christian belief that Adam and Eve existed in the best possible human state of existence before the Fall or the common conservative belief that heaven is the best possible state of existence for those who no longer have an earthly existence. Those who hold such beliefs are not arguing that Adam and Eve could not, for example, have experienced a greater degree of happiness in their prelapsarian state, or that those in heaven could not, for example, experience an even more fulfilling state of existence. The implicit assumption, rather, is that Adam and Eve experienced, and those in heaven are experiencing, an ideal (or best) type of existence.[14]

But even if (M4) is interpreted in this sense, that is, even if we interpret the requirement that God maximize the quality of life on earth as the requirement that God do all he can within the legitimate constraints of this world to actualize an ideal state of existence for each person, is this a principle that a freewill theist must (or should) affirm?

All agree that if God is an act utilitarian (is obligated to "maximize happiness and/or minimize suffering" in each "particular case"[15]), the answer is yes. That is, all agree that if God acts in accordance with this mode of ethical decision-making, then God must do all that can be done to maximize the quality of life (make life ideal). But in two important and influential essays Robert Adams denies that this is necessarily the case if God is not an act utilitarian.[16] As long as an individual's existence is on the whole worth living, he argues, a non-act utilitarian God is not obligated to do more.[17]

It is first important to note the limited relevance of Adams's contention. His claim is conditional: a non-act utilitarian God need not maximize (or even attempt to maximize) the quality of life for an individual *if* that individual's existence is on the whole worth living. But, as we have seen, if the God of BFWT does not have MK, then God is not normally in a position to know all that will happen to any individual before deciding what to do for that individual. Specifically, God is not normally in a position to know whether any individual's life will on the whole be worth living before deciding at any given point whether to do all that can be done to increase the quality of life for that individual. Accordingly, Adams's critique of (M4) cannot be directly utilized by those freewill theists who do in fact deny that God possesses MK (and do not assume that God will, when necessary, unilaterally ensure in an afterlife a life worth living).[18]

But what if we assume that God has always known (or comes to know at a given point) that a person's existence will on the whole be worth living? Is it then true, as Adams believes, that if God is a non-act utilitarian, God is justified in doing less for that person than what could have been done?

In defense of his contention, Adams attempts to respond to what he sees as the two major non-act utilitarian objections:

(5) "A creator would necessarily wrong someone (violate someone's rights), or be less kind to someone than a perfectly good moral agent must be, if he knowingly created [a world in which he had not chosen to do what he could have done to maximize the

quality of life for all individuals therein]."

(6) "Even if no one would be wronged or treated unkindly by the creation of [a world in which God had not chosen to maximize the quality of life for all individuals], the creator's choice of [such] a world must manifest a defect in character."[19]

Adams's most recent criticism of (5) can be summarized as follows. If those natural and physical evils that occurred prior to our existence or that we have personally experienced in the past had not occurred, we would not be the same individuals we are today. But it is better to have an existence that is on the whole satisfying or worth living than to have no existence at all. Therefore, if our lives are on the whole satisfying, we cannot claim that God has been less than omnibenevolent by causing or permitting us to experience certain evils, even if this world is one in which God has, for whatever reasons, chosen to do less than God could have done to maximize our quality of life.[20]

When Adams claims that we would not be the same people we are if our past history had been significantly different, he means that

> the farther back we go in history, the larger the proportion of evils to which we owe our being; for the causal nexus relevant to our individual genesis widens as we go back in time. We almost certainly would never have existed had there not been just about the same evils as actually occurred in a large part of human history. . . . We may ask why God does not intervene in the natural historical process in our lifetime to protect us from the consequences of [evil]. . . . There are evils that happen to people, without which they could, strictly speaking, have existed, but which shape their lives so profoundly that wishing the evils had not occurred would be morally very close to wishing that somebody else had existed instead of those particular people.[21]

To illustrate how this concept of "sameness" functions in the current context, Adams discusses the life of Helen Keller. Keller, Adams believes, lived on the whole a happy and satisfying life, even though her life contained much pain and sorrow. But let us assume, he argues, that Helen Keller had not been rendered blind and deaf by a fever at nineteen months of age and that she would have led a better, happier life as a result. "Would it have been reasonable for Helen Keller, as an adult, to wish, for her own sake, that she had never been blind or deaf?" Adams thinks not. "Her actual life . . . was built around the fact of her blindness and deafness. That other, happier life would have contained few of the particular joys and sorrows, trials and triumphs . . . that she cared about in her actual life." Accordingly, Adams concludes, "her never having been blind would have been very like her never having existed," and "why should she wish for that," given that she lived on the whole a satisfying existence?[22] In other words, as Adams sees it, since Helen Keller's life was on the whole worth living, it cannot be maintained that God was unfair or less than kind to her, even if God could have brought it about that she would not have had the damaging fever at nineteen months of age and even if her life would have been happier (of a higher quality) as a result.

Such reasoning, however, is far from convincing. It may be true that *if* God is not an act utilitarian, God cannot be accused of having wronged Helen Keller *solely* because of having failed to maximize her happiness. But it is not at all clear to me that God cannot in this context be accused of having wronged Helen Keller, even if he is not an act utilitarian and did bring it about that her life was on the whole worth living.

My basis for complaint can be illustrated by an analogous hypothetical scenario. Assume that a man named Jones knows that his son has an interest in medicine and has no doubt that his son could become a doctor and in this capacity lead a very satisfying, fulfilling life. Let us also assume that Jones wants his son to become part of the family business and has no doubt that if his son does so, he will lead a satisfying life, although not as satisfying as the life that he would lead if he became a doctor. Finally, let us assume that Jones's influence over his son is such that his son will in fact do whatever he wants him to do. Has Jones wronged his son if he brings it about that he becomes a part of the family business?

Of course, given a non-act utilitarian perspective, Jones cannot be accused of having wronged his son solely because he did not maximize his son's quality of life. But such a response, I believe, simply misses the point. The basic moral question here is not the maximization of value for the son. Nor is it the nature of the son's subsequent life history. The basic moral issue at hand, as I see it, centers on the following principle:

(7) One ought not knowingly and voluntarily attempt to diminish the quality of life (happiness, satisfaction, actualization of desired ends) experienced by another person over whose life one has control solely (or even primarily) for the purpose of satisfying one's own desires.

Of course, if Jones does not really have control over his son's actions or if he truly believes that some greater good for all concerned will be brought about if he convinces his son to stay at home or if he does not consciously acknowledge the true nature of his intent, (7) is not applicable. But if Jones knowingly and voluntarily brings it about that his son leads a less satisfying existence solely (or even primarily) for his own benefit, then, given (7), Jones can rightly be said to have wronged his son, regardless of his son's own ultimate assessment of his life history. For given (7), it is the intent of the person performing an action, not the consequences of the action, that determines its moral status.

Likewise, given (7), God can rightly be said to have wronged Helen Keller, *the healthy nineteen-month-old child*, if God caused or permitted her to have the fever that rendered her deaf and blind solely (or even primarily) to satisfy God's own desires. The fact that she subsequently lived a meaningful, satisfying life becomes irrelevant. So the crucial question in relation to (5), the contention that God necessarily wrongs someone by doing less than could have been done, is whether (7) is a principle that the freewill theist must (or ought to) affirm. Can the God of BFWT do less for someone than could be done primarily to satisfy his own desires?

It seems to me that (7) ought to be affirmed, especially by a Judeo-Christian freewill theist. The violator of (7) appears to me to be a paradigmatic example of a person whose actions are inconsistent with Christ's command to "love your neighbor as yourself" or his exhortation that "as you would have men do to you, do also to them" or with the apostle Paul's claim that love "seeketh not its own." In short, the violator of (7) appears to me to be a paradigmatic example of the type of selfish individual that the Christian canon condemns.

However, there is nothing inherent in BFWT, as I see it, that *requires* a freewill theist to affirm (7). Thus while I deny adamantly that those freewill theists who believe that God possesses MK must agree with Adams that (5) is false (must agree that a non-act utilitarian God has not wronged us by not having done all that he can to maximize our quality of life), I also deny that such freewill theists cannot agree with Adams on this point.

But what of (6), the other major non-act utilitarian objection to Adams's thesis? Is it not the case that the divine actualization of a world in which God has chosen not to do all that he can for all inhabitants would necessarily manifest a defect in God's character? In response to this challenge, Adams offers the following argument:

> One important element in the Judaeo-Christian moral ideal is *grace*. For present purposes, grace may be defined as a disposition to love which is not dependent on the merit of the person loved. . . . A God who is gracious with respect to creating might well choose to create and love less excellent creatures than he

could have chosen. This is not to suggest that grace in creation consists in a preference for imperfection as such. God could have chosen to create the best of all possible creatures, and still have been gracious in choosing them. . . . It implies, rather, that even if they are the best possible creatures, that is not the ground for his choosing them. And it implies that there is nothing in God's nature or character which would require Him to act on the principle of choosing the best possible creatures to be the object of his creative powers.[23]

Adams's terminology differs slightly from that which we have been using, but the essence of his argument seems to be that since a gracious God can love equally individuals of any given sort (for example, can love those who suffer as much as those who do not), God is not obligated to create individuals of any sort (for example, is not obligated to create individuals whose quality of life has been maximized).

I personally find this line of reasoning totally unconvincing in that it seems to confuse the important distinction between the *reasons* that a being might choose to express its love to other beings and the *manner in which* such love should be expressed. It may well be, for example, that a gracious parent can (or even ought to) love the child who is physically or mentally handicapped as much as the child who has no such condition. To be gracious in this sense is simply to express love in an unconditional (agapeic) manner, and such graciousness is, of course, quite compatible with Judeo-Christian thought (as well as the tenets of the other major world religions).

But the fact that a gracious parent can (or even ought to) love all children equally does not necessarily mean that he or she can justifiably express love for (treat) a child in a manner that does not maximize this child's quality of life. On the contrary, it seems to me that the truly good parent, even if gracious, is required to do all that he or she can to help any child with problems lead a life that is as productive and enjoyable as possible.

The same, I feel, is true in relation to God. It is certainly consistent with Judeo-Christian thought to argue that God is gracious in the sense that God can love equally individuals of any sort, for this is simply to say that God's love is unconditional. But it does not follow from the fact that a gracious God can love equally individuals of any sort that, as a perfectly good being, God can also express love for them in a manner that does not maximize their quality of life. For example, it does not follow from the fact that a gracious God can love those who are mentally impaired as much as those who are not that God is not obligated, as a perfectly good being, to do what he can to help impaired individuals overcome their handicaps. Rather, as I see it, a God who is perfectly good is required, even if "gracious," to do everything possible to help those in need.

However, although I personally believe for this reason that (6) is true (that for God to do less than he can for us does manifest a defect in God's character), I find nothing inherent in BFWT that requires proponents to agree with me. They can, I again acknowledge, agree with Adams.

Accordingly, we must conclude that Adams's contention that God need not to the extent possible maximize the quality of life for each of us (his critique of [M4]) is *in a limited sense* successful. His critique is not available to a freewill theist who denies that God possesses MK (which is ironic, since it does not appear that Adams himself believes God possesses MK). Nor is any freewill theist required to agree with Adams—required to agree that a perfectly good non-act utilitarian God can do less than can be done for us if God has ensured that our lives are on balance worth living. However, there is, as I see it, nothing inherent in BFWT that prohibits a freewill theist who believes God has MK from adopting Adams's perspective.[24]

What if a freewill theist believes, though, that God does not possess MK and thus that God does not know, when making decisions, if the existence of each person who may be affected by these decisions will on the whole be worth living? Should this freewill theist then maintain that God must at least do everything possible to maximize the quality of life for each individual?

As I see it, there is nothing inherent in BFWT that would require a proponent to affirm (M4) in this case. But there is also certainly nothing inherent in BFWT that would prohibit a freewill theist from doing so. In fact, it might appear that it would be quite reasonable for a freewill theist who does not believe God can guarantee a world in which all have on balance lives worth living to maintain that God must at least do all that he can.

However, one notable freewill theist, William Hasker, believes that it is unwise for *any* theist to affirm (M4) (to maintain that God must attempt to maximize the quality of life for all) in *any* context.[25] In a response to my original critique of Adams, Hasker agrees that (M4) is "logically coherent and is not open to the charge that it proposes an impossible task for God." He even grants that "it is not lacking in initial plausibility."[26] But Hasker believes that this creative obligation is incompatible with the reality of natural evil and for this reason ought to be rejected.

To illustrate his point, he refers again to the fever that left Helen Keller blind and deaf at nineteen months of age. If we maintain that God must do all he can to maximize each person's quality of life, we are then left to assume, Hasker points out, that Keller's fever was "an undesired, but unavoidable, by-product of the significant freedom and/or natural laws which operate in this world." But it is most unlikely, he claims, "that Helen Keller's fever and disability were the direct consequence of a free choice made by some person such that God could not have prevented the disability without depriving that person of significant freedom." Nor, as Hasker sees it, would God's direct intervention in this case have disrupted the natural laws on which free choice is based, since "God could have intervened so as to leave Helen with only a slight hearing impairment without anyone's becoming aware of this intervention." Accordingly, Hasker concludes that the theist who claims that God must attempt to maximize the quality of life for all (who affirms [M4]) is left with a theodicy that "ends rather unhappily." In response to natural evil such a theist will be "quickly reduced to a stone-walling mode of defense in which he maintains on *a priori* grounds a view which runs against the grain of universal human experience."[27]

But what is Hasker's alternative for the theist? It is to drop (M4) with its inherent requirement that God always exercise "meticulous providence—that is, a providence in which all events are carefully controlled and manipulated in such a way that no evils are permitted to occur except as they are necessary for the production of a greater good." Rather, theists should "promote an understanding of God's dealing with the world according to which God can, and indeed does, permit very considerable amounts of gratuitous evil in the course of pursuing his overall plan for the world."[28]

Unfortunately, Hasker's criticism is based in part on a common confusion. The contention that an evil state of affairs is outweighed by a related good can be given two distinct readings:

(8) The good that is *produced* by a particular occurrence of evil outweighs this evil;

and,

(9) The good that *makes possible* a particular occurrence of evil outweighs the evil.

When Hasker claims that the proponent of (M4) must affirm meticulous providence, that is, must believe that all permitted evils are "necessary for the production of a greater good," he is making it appear that the proponent of (M4) (the person who believes God must attempt to maximize each person's quality of life) must evaluate all natural evil in terms of (8). That is, he is making it appear that the affirmation of (M4) requires the theist to maintain that an omnibenevolent God can allow a person to experience evil only when such evil will produce some particular good that outweighs this evil and cannot be produced without it. But this is not so.

The proponent of (M4) may plausibly attempt to explain some natural evil in terms of (8). She may, for example, agree with John Hick that God allows some individuals to experience some natural evil to build their character. But she need not always (or even usually) do so. She can also analyze natural evil in terms of (9). That is, a person who believes that God must do everything possible to maximize the quality of life for all can readily admit that many of the natural evils humans experience *do not produce* a greater good for anyone, maintaining instead that the intrinsic good generated by the creation of a context in which individuals can make meaningful free choices or experience moral or emotional growth outweighs the instances of intrinsically unnecessary evil that this context allows. In short, once we clearly distinguish, as Hasker does not, between (8) and (9), we see that the concept of meticulous providence offers no basis for the rejection of (M4).

Another aspect of Hasker's criticism, however, remains to be considered. He is correct in arguing that most proponents of (M4) (most who believe that God must attempt to maximize everyone's quality of life) will admit that God can (and does) at times directly manipulate human decision-making and/or the natural environment to lessen the impact of certain evils or generate certain goods. Thus with respect to any given instance of natural or moral evil, it is reasonable to ask the proponent of (M4) why God did not beneficially intervene. And it is true, as Hasker says, that the proponent of (M4) will not always have a convincing answer—that is, will not always have an explanation that makes it clear to all why God could not have unilaterally removed the evil in question without significantly upsetting the intrinsically valuable context of freedom and growth in which God wants humans to function.

But will it help the concerned theist to deny, as Hasker suggests, that God is obligated to attempt to maximize everyone's quality of life? This does provide another possible explanation for the seemingly unnecessary natural evil that we experience, namely, that God is under no obligation to remove such evil even if he can. But what does such a response say about God's moral integrity? I agree with George Schlesinger's contention that we should "apply as far as possible human ethical standards in our appraisal of Divine conduct"[29] since "we have no other notions of good and bad except those appertaining to human situations."[30] And it seems clear to me that we as humans generally do believe that we should do what we can to maximize the quality of life for others, especially when those "others" are children whom we have brought into existence. Accordingly, my question for those who would have the theist deny (M4) is, Why should anyone desire to worship or expect nontheists to respect the concept of a being who appears not to be obligated to act as morally as some humans?

Responses that will satisfy some theists may exist. Hasker, for example, seems to feel that a proper understanding of the concept of divine grace allows God to escape adherence to (M4).[31] But any such response, I believe, will be no more satisfying to the nontheist or to the majority of theists than will the response that proponents of (M4) must give to instances of seemingly unnecessary evil. It seems to me, in fact, that the burden of proposing an explanation for natural evil that preserves God's moral integrity is even greater if the theist, following Hasker's advice, denies that God must do everything possible to maximize each person's quality of life. Consequently, I deny that Hasker gives freewill theists a good reason to reject (M4).[32] In fact, I believe that the considerations I have offered in response furnish freewill theists, especially those who deny that God can guarantee a world in which all experience a good life on balance, with good (although not logically compelling) reasons to affirm (M4).

However, even if a freewill theist denies that God must attempt to maximize the quality of life for all, ought not he or she at least affirm either (M2*) (the contention that God must always attempt to recompense innocent suffering to the extent possible) or (M3*) (the contention that God must attempt to ensure that every person has a life that is on the whole worth living)? It seems to me that the answer is yes, and most freewill theists clearly agree. Some, however, may not, and I see nothing inherent in BFWT that requires freewill theists to affirm even these minimal obligatory principles.

There is, though, an interesting relationship between (M3*) and (M4) that should be noted at this point. To affirm (M3*) is to maintain that God will attempt to make the life of each individual on the whole worth living. But, as noted previously, a God who does not have MK does not know (or normally know) when deciding how to treat an individual whether this individual's life will actually be on the whole worth living. Accordingly, it is questionable whether a God who is under the obligation outlined in (M3*) but does not possess MK could ever be (or at least often be) in a position to do less than could be done for an individual since to do so might in the final analysis bring it about (or at least increase the possibility) that this person's life would not be on the whole worth living. That is, it is questionable whether a freewill theist who affirms (M3*) but denies that God possesses MK can reject (M4)—can deny that God must attempt to maximize the quality of life for all.

Conclusion

The purpose of this chapter has been to identify the moral principles that freewill theists can, must or do believe serve as a basis for divine decision-making. We found that freewill theists who believe that God possesses MK *can* place God under any of the obligations noted, including the obligation to create the "best" actualizable world. We also found that while freewill theists who deny that God possesses MK cannot maintain that God is obligated to actualize the best actualizable world or to create a world in which God does in fact prevent all preventable evil or does in fact ensure that each person will have an existence that is on the whole worth living or does in fact maximize the quality of life for each individual, they *can* maintain that God is obligated to attempt to bring about these states of affairs.

On the other hand, there is nothing inherent in BFWT (or theism in general) that *requires* freewill theists to place God under any of these obligations. But all freewill theists do as a matter of fact believe that God is at least obligated to attempt to prevent all preventable suffering (suffering that can be removed without negatively affecting God's creative goals). And most believe that God is also obligated to attempt to recompense innocent sufferers, ensure lives that are on the whole worth living and in other ways maximize the quality of life for each individual.

4
BASIC
FREEWILL
THEISM & EVIL

AS POINTED OUT IN CHAPTER THREE, ONE OF THE CHALLENGES facing any theist is the tremendous amount of seemingly unnecessary evil in the world. The purpose of this chapter is to assess the relationship between basic freewill theism (BFWT)[1] and evil, with the goal of determining whether evil does in fact present an insurmountable problem for proponents of this theistic perspective.

Many (if not most) philosophical discussions of the relationship between God and evil continue to be based on the assumption that *all* theists who believe that God is omnipotent and perfectly good face the *same* prima facie challenge, which may be summarized as follows:

(1) An omnipotent being could ensure that no evil occurred.

(2) A perfectly good being would never desire (seek to bring about) the occurrence of evil.

(3) Evil occurs in our world.

Therefore,

who is omnipotent and perfectly good.

However, the assumption that this is a challenge faced by all theists of the type in question is in an important sense misguided.[2] It is certainly true that all individuals who hold the same or very similar beliefs on any issue are equally subject to whatever tensions the affirmation of those beliefs might produce. However, as we have seen in the previous chapters, it is simply not the case that all theists (even all freewill theists) who believe that God is omnipotent and perfectly good hold the same, or even similar, beliefs concerning the nature and extent of God's power or the value that a perfectly good being places on various states of affairs. Nor do all theists even agree on the types of evil that exist. Accordingly, the challenge outlined above is of little value in helping us determine whether evil actually does pose a serious problem for theism.

As a number of philosophers are coming to realize, in order to determine whether evil actually poses a challenge to any given theist, it is necessary to identify the exact sense in which this theist believes that God is omnipotent and perfectly good and then assess whether belief in the existence of a being with these characteristics is compatible with the belief that this world contains the amount and types of evil that this theist acknowledges it does.[3] What happens when we approach the relationship between the God of BFWT and evil in this fashion? Do we find that evil poses a serious problem for proponents of this perspective?

Evil Defined

Before considering this question, it is important to examine briefly the concept of evil itself. What exactly is evil? Specifically, what categorizations of evil are relevant in this context? Philosophers have had a very difficult time achieving consensus regarding the definition of "evil." Some simply give examples of actual states of affairs they believe deserve this label. Michael Peterson, for example, offers the following list: "extreme pain and suffering, physical deformities, psychological abnormalities, the prosperity of bad men, the demise of good men, disrupted social relations, unfulfilled potential, a host of character defects and natural catastrophes."[4] Any such list of "evils," however, stimulates the question, What characteristic(s) do these concrete examples share? Furthermore, evil is never discussed generically in philosophical circles. Distinctions are always made. So it is important that I attempt to specify as clearly as possible exactly what it is that I believe all evils have in common and exactly how these evils are to be categorized. As I see it, what is common to the states of affairs that most identify as evil is that they are *inherently undesirable* in the sense that these states of affairs, *in and of themselves,* not only lack inherent value but actually detract from or diminish the value in our world; they are states of affairs that themselves have "negative value."[5]

There are, though, at least two situations in which most of us believe it is justifiable for humans to bring about or to allow evils (inherently undesirable states of affairs). We recognize that humans are sometimes forced to perform or to allow evil acts because such states of affairs are *necessary antecedent conditions* for the actualization of desirable goals or ends. For example, we understand that parents at times need to discipline their children (do things that are inherently undesirable) for the sake of developing their children's character (a good end). Second, we also recognize that some evils are *unnecessary but unavoidable byproducts* of desirable goals or ends that humans attempt to bring about. Consider, for example, the parent who doubts that many of the painful experiences her "special needs" child must endure at school—the taunting and the abuse—will lead to any greater good but sends the child to school anyway because she believes it is absolutely crucial that her child receive an education. The inherently undesirable states of affairs in this case (the painful experiences) are not necessary antecedent causal conditions for the actualization of the desired goal (her child's education). But to the extent that such experiences really are unavoidable byproducts of the educational process in question, most of us would not consider this mother morally blameworthy for allowing such evils to occur.

However, we also recognize that individuals sometimes bring about or allow evil that cannot be justified in either of the two ways described above. Such evil, which I shall label *excess* evil, does count against the moral character of the person who causes or allows it. For example, sexual abuse is neither a necessary condition for, or an unavoidable byproduct of, caring for children and thus, as excess evil, is appropriately considered to count against the moral character of the perpetrator.

These same distinctions, not surprisingly, often arise in discussions of the relationship between God and evil. Few theists deny the reality of evil, but all deny that any of the evil we experience is excess. Every instance of evil, it is held, is either a *necessary antecedent condition for*, or the *unavoidable byproduct of*, the actualization of God's creative goals and thus is not incompatible with his existence. Critics of theistic belief, on the other hand, almost always maintain that because some of the evil in this world is clearly neither "necessary" nor "unavoidable," it is *excess* and thus incompatible with God's existence. Unfortunately, there exists no standard terminology for these three categories of evil, and current discussions often blur the distinctions in question. Phrases such as "gratuitous evil," "genuine evil," "real evil," "surplus evil" and "unabsorbed evil" are used by some to refer exclusively to what I am labeling excess evil (evil that an omnipotent, perfectly good being could and would have prevented), while others include under these headings both excess evil and evil that is unnecessary but unavoidable.[6]

In an attempt to avoid such ambiguity, I will divide evil into three categories. That evil which is a logically necessary antecedent condition for the actualization of God's creative goals will be labeled *necessary evil*; that evil which, while not a locally necessary condition for the actualization of God's creative goals, is an unavoidable byproduct of the actualization of these goals will be labeled *unavoidable evil;* and that evil which an all-powerful and perfectly good God would and could prevent will be labeled *excess evil.*

Basic Explanation for Evil

The fundamental question is, Can proponents of BFWT—hereafter referred to as freewill theists—avoid the charge that this world contains excess evil? To answer this question, we must first consider (reconsider in more detail) the basic explanation for evil inherent in BFWT. Freewill theists, like most theists, acknowledge the reality of some necessary evil—some evil that is a necessary condition for the actualization of some divine goal. Unlike theological determinists, however, freewill theists deny that God can actualize unilaterally just any logically possible (compossible) state of affairs. Specifically, as incompatibilists, they deny that God can grant us meaningful freedom—the ability to bring about both good and evil—and yet unilaterally control the decision-making process in such a way that we will always make the exact decisions God would have us make, even in those cases where it is logically possible that we do so.

Furthermore, freewill theists believe that human decision-making (and the natural environmental context it requires) is capable of producing unavoidable evil—instances of evil that, although not necessary antecedent conditions for the actualization of God's desire for individuals to exercise meaningful freedom, are unavoidable byproducts of the actualization of this creative goal. Accordingly, since freewill theists believe that God did choose to create a world containing individuals who possess significant freedom, they acknowledge that this world may well contain unavoidable, as well as necessary, evil.

Freewill theists, however, deny that God had (has) knowledge of any world (or even type of world) that could have been initiated (or brought into being now) that would better satisfy God's creative goals.[7] In short, they deny that this world contains any evil that God could remove and yet allows. Hence, they conclude that the evil in this world is not incompatible with the existence of the perfectly good, all-powerful being to whom they give allegiance, even if this world does contain many states of affairs that are inherently undesirable.[8] Is this explanation of evil adequate? Does it allow the freewill theist to successfully counter the critic's claim that some of the evil in our world is excess and thus incompatible with the existence of God? The answer to this question depends in part on what is being asked.

It has become popular in recent discussions of evil to distinguish between a theodicy and a defense.[9] A theodicy is an attempt to offer plausible explanations for the evil we experience—that is, an attempt to identify plausible reasons that a perfectly good God would cause or would allow the evil in our world. As such, the assessment of a theodicy requires the consideration of theistic truth claims. A defense, on the other hand, simply attempts to demonstrate that the assertions "God is omnipotent, omniscient and wholly good" and "Evil exists" are not inconsistent propositions. To offer a successful defense, one need only identify a set of propositions that when conjoined with "A good God exists" entails that "Evil exists," propositions that, as Alvin Plantinga has rightly noted, "clearly . . . need be neither true, nor probable, nor plausible, nor believed by most theists, nor anything else of that sort."[10]

Consequently, since the relationship between God and evil outlined by freewill theists contains propositions believed to be not only plausible but true, it is clear that freewill theists are not simply offering us a logical defense—not simply arguing that simultaneous belief in God and evil cannot be shown to be logically incompatible. We are being offered a theodicy. We are being told why freewill theists believe God's existence can be affirmed, even if the reality of evil is granted.[11]

There are, though, two types of theodicies. A theist can attempt to offer an explanation for evil that she believes no rational individual can deny or an explanation that she believes she herself can reasonably affirm, even if others can justifiably disagree. Applied to our situation, this means that when freewill theists maintain that belief in God is compatible with the reality of evil, they could be arguing either that no rational person can deny that the evil in this world is compatible with the existence of the God of BFWT or that a freewill theist can herself coherently deny that the evil in this world is incompatible with the existence of the God of BFWT.

As I see it, there is nothing inherent in BFWT that would prohibit a freewill theist from making either claim. But the vast majority of freewill theists have wished only to defend their epistemic right to simultaneous belief in God and evil. Accordingly, it is on this contention that our discussion will be focused, which in turn means that the central question related to the adequacy of the freewill response to evil becomes the following: Can freewill theists justifiably maintain that this world contains no excess evil (and thus that the evil in this world is compatible with the existence of the God of BFWT)?

Some philosophers have claimed that there is an important sense in which no freewill theist can deny the reality of excess evil. However, before considering these challenges, it is important to assess William Hasker's contention that those freewill theists who deny that God possesses middle knowledge (MK) are in a much stronger (more reasonable, more plausible) position to deny the existence of excess evil than those who maintain that God does possess this form of omniscience.[12]

Evil and Middle Knowledge

If God possesses MK, Hasker informs us, then he intentionally brings about each event that actually occurs. He "specifically planned the Holocaust, Saddam Hussein's invasion of Kuwait,

[and] the ethnic cleansing in Bosnia." But this in turn means, Hasker adds, that to preserve God's goodness, the freewill theist who affirms MK must also acknowledge that God possesses meticulous providence—that is, acknowledge "that every single instance of evil that occurs is such that God's permitting either that specific evil or some other equal or greater evil is necessary for some greater good which is better than anything God could have brought about without permitting the evil in question." And "it strains one's credulity almost beyond limits," we are told, "to believe that none of the evils mentioned—or a thousand more that could have been added—could have been prevented without creating an even greater evil, or without losing some good that is great enough to outweigh those truly horrendous evils."[13]

On the other hand, Hasker continues, if the God of BFWT does not possess MK, then while he "knows that evils will occur . . . he has not for the most part specifically decreed or incorporated into his plan the individual instances of evil,"[14] which means in turn that a freewill theist who denies that God possesses MK need not maintain that God exercises meticulous providence. She can maintain, instead, that God exercises only general providence. That is, she can maintain that "God adopts certain *overall strategies* in his dealing with the world . . . *strategies* [that] are justified in that they enable the creation of great and significant goods" but "also permit the occurrence of *individual instances* of evil which are, as such, pure loss and *not* the means to any greater good."[15] And to be able to conceive of the relationship between God and the world in this manner, Hasker concludes, places the freewill theist who rejects MK in a much better position "to compose a strong and plausible reply to the problem of evil."[16]

Hasker's argument seems plausible initially, but it is, I believe, based on a flawed assumption. Hasker presupposes that the freewill theist who believes that God possesses MK is committed to the belief that each instance of evil that God allows is permitted because that evil is a required means to some good state of affairs that outweighs it. Or, to utilize the categories set forth earlier, it is Hasker's contention that the freewill theist who believes that God possesses MK must maintain that all evil is *necessary* (that each instance of evil is a necessary antecedent condition for the actualization of God's creative goals).[17] This contention, however, is false. As we saw in chapter two, it is true that a God with MK knows exactly what voluntary choices individuals will make in any given context before they make them. And it is true that he can unilaterally determine who will exercise voluntary choice and in what contexts they can do so. Thus it is true that a God who possesses MK may at times be able to ensure that individuals will voluntarily make the exact decisions he would have them make simply by placing them in contexts in which he foreknows that they will make the desired choices. However, since a God with MK cannot ensure that there will always exist actualizable contexts of this sort, it is also true that God may not at times be able to ensure that individuals will voluntarily make the exact decisions he would have them make.[18]

Consequently, since all freewill theists believe that human decision-making (and the natural environmental context it requires) is capable of producing unavoidable evil (instances of evil that, although not necessary antecedent conditions for the actualization of God's desire for individuals to exercise meaningful freedom, are unavoidable byproducts of the actualization of this creative goal), freewill theists who maintain that God possesses MK need not maintain that each instance of evil God allows is permitted because it is a required means to greater good—a necessary condition for some good—that outweighs it.

Freewill theists who affirm MK, like those who deny that God possesses MK, can maintain that God chose to create a world containing evil that is "pure loss" because the good inherent in a world containing individuals who exercise free choice (even with disastrous results at times) outweighs this evil. That is, freewill theists who believe that God possesses MK, like those who do not, can maintain that God exercises general (as opposed to meticulous) providence, and thus that this world contains unavoidable, as well as necessary, evil. The only difference is that a God with MK *knew before creation* what evil he would cause or allow while a God without MK *knows now* what evil he is causing or allowing.

Moreover, this difference can actually be viewed as favoring a God with MK. If God has MK, then he knew before creation exactly how much evil he would be allowing if he actualized this world, and we can, therefore, be assured that he has decided that this evil will ultimately be outweighed by the good for which it is a necessary condition and/or the good inherent in significant freedom. However, if God does not have MK, then this may not be the case. Unless a God without MK has decided that the good inherent in significant freedom itself outweighs any amount of evil that the use of this freedom might generate in our world, he is not in a position to know what the ultimate balance between good and evil will be.[19] Hence, at the very least, the absence of MK gives God no advantage in responding to evil, as Hasker maintains.[20]

The Inductive Challenge

Let us turn our attention then to those who challenge the right of any freewill theist to deny the reality of excess evil in our world. Few if any critics of BFWT argue today that it is logically impossible for the freewill theist to deny that this world contains any excess evil—to deny that the propositions "God exists" (in the sense acknowledged by freewill theists) and "This world contains no excess evil" are necessarily inconsistent. As William Alston notes, "It is now acknowledged on (almost) all sides that the logical argument is bankrupt."[21]

But many do continue to claim that the likelihood (probability) that this world contains excess evil is so great that freewill theists cannot reasonably deny the reality of such evil (and thus cannot reasonably affirm the existence of their God).[22] Such challenges to BFWT may differ in detail, but they all include some version of the following line of reasoning.

(5) What appears to be the case is prima facie justification for believing it to be the case.

(6) It clearly appears to be the case (i.e., there is a plausible basis for assuming) that a being with the acknowledged power, moral character and creative goals of the God of BFWT would not allow as much evil as we experience in our world.

(7) Therefore, we have prima facie justification for believing that a being with the acknowledged power, moral character and creative goals of the God of BFWT would not allow as much evil as we experience in our world.

(8) Unless there exist counterbalancing reasons for rejecting a belief for which we have prima facie justification, the rejection of this belief is not justified.

(9) No one (including no freewill theist) can justifiably maintain that there exist counterbalancing (sufficient, equally plausible) reasons for rejecting the belief that a being with the acknowledged power, moral character and creative goals of the God of BFWT would not allow as much evil as we experience in our world.

(10) Therefore, the freewill theist cannot justifiably deny that this world contains *excess* evil (and thus justifiably deny that the evil in this world is incompatible with the God of BFWT).

Response to the Inductive Challenge

Most philosophers, including most theistic philosophers, accept some version of (5), which Richard Swinburne labels the "principle of credulity."[23] Therefore we will turn our attention to (6), the contention that it clearly appears to be the case that a being with the acknowledged power, moral character and creative goals of the God of BFWT would not allow as much evil as we experience in our world.

The arguments supporting this claim fall into two basic categories. Proponents of what I label the *functional challenge* allow (for the sake of argument) what freewill theists identify as God's creative goals but deny that the actualization of such goals requires the types and amounts of evil we experience. It may be true, it is acknowledged, that the God of BFWT cannot both grant individuals meaningful freedom and ensure that this world will contain no natural or moral evil. However, the God of BFWT possesses the acknowledged power to prevent any natural disaster—those cancers, tidal waves, floods and the like that cause so much suffering to innocent people. Moreover, it certainly appears that God could beneficially utilize this power in crucial contexts to a greater extent than he does without negatively affecting the significant freedom he desires that we exercise—that is, without negatively affecting this important divine goal. It certainly appears, for instance, that God could destroy a cancer cell or modify slightly the course of a tornado at a crucial moment without negatively affecting our ability to exercise significant freedom overall.

Furthermore, the God of BFWT possesses the acknowledged power and right to prevent us from exercising our freedom in some contexts. And it certainly seems that God could also utilize this power in crucial contexts to a greater extent than he does without negatively affecting the significant freedom he desires we exercise, that is, without negatively affecting this important divine goal. It appears, for instance, that God could have withdrawn Hitler's freedom at crucial moments without negatively affecting his ability to exercise significant freedom overall. As critic David Griffin acknowledges, in those moments "the apparent human beings would not really be humans, if 'humans' are by definition free." But this, he continues, "would seem to be a small price to pay if some of the world's worst evils could be averted."[24]

Thus the proponent of the functional challenge concludes that even if the God of BFWT cannot control free choice, (6) is clearly true—there clearly exists a plausible basis for assuming that *some* of the natural and/or moral evil in our world is excess.[25] In fact, states critic William Rowe, "in light of our experience and knowledge of the variety and scale of human and animal suffering in our world, the idea that none of the instances of suffering could have been prevented by [a being with the acknowledged properties of the God of BFWT] . . . seems an extraordinary, absurd idea, quite beyond our belief."[26]

Other proponents of (6) grant for the sake of argument that the actualization of the creative goals in question might require God to allow the evil we experience but deny that a perfectly good being would create a world on the basis of goals that would require that being to allow such evil. Advocates of this line of reasoning, which I label the *moral challenge*, acknowledge that each instance of evil in this world is either a logically necessary antecedent condition for or an unavoidable byproduct of the creative goals that the God of BFWT is said to possess *in this world*. But it is hard to imagine, they contend, that a being who was *perfectly good* would ever consider the satisfaction of any set of creative goals to be an adequate basis for the creation of (or at least the continuation of) a world containing as much horrific evil as we find in this world. It is hard to imagine, for example, that such a being would consider the satisfaction of any set of creative goals a reasonable basis for allowing the Holocaust or the brutal murders of tens of thousands of small children or the mental torment endured by tens of millions or the horrors of starvation experienced by hundreds of millions.[27]

It seems, rather, that a good God would have created a different type of world, one in which his creative activity was motivated by creative goals that would not require him to cause or to allow the occurrence of as much horrific evil. It is reasonable to assume, for example, that God would have created a world with sentient beings who only thought they were free or a world in which the natural order was not as hostile to human life. So even if this world does contain only necessary and unavoidable evil, given God's goals, it must still be acknowledged, concludes the moral critic, that some of the evil in this world appears to be excess (that [6] is true).[28]

Freewill theists have offered at least three types of response to the functional challenge (the claim that the God of BFWT could actualize his creative goals with less evil). Some question what they see as the implicit assumption in this contention: "God's ways are enough like our ways" for us to determine with any degree of confidence what a supernatural being who was perfectly good would in fact do in most contexts. It may well appear *to us*, these freewill theists acknowledge, that if *we* had the power, moral character and creative goals of the God of BFWT, we could and would prevent some of the evil we experience. But we as finite beings are not in a position to know (or even to understand) what an infinite being might do and why. "Our cognitive powers, as opposed to God's," as Plantinga tells us, "are a bit slim for that."[29] Thus, they conclude, no freewill theist need grant that there exists a plausible basis for maintaining that the God of BFWT would actually do more (need grant [6]).[30]

Other freewill theists acknowledge our ability to identify *specific* "free choices" or natural occurrences that God seemingly could have vetoed or modified without negatively affecting his creative goals, that is, some acknowledge the prima facie plausibility of the functional challenge when applied to natural occurrences or "free choices" in isolation. But what the proponent of (6) must demonstrate, these freewill theists argue, is something that is much more difficult to establish in an objective manner: that it is plausible to assume that the different world system of which such interventions would be a part would allow for the actualization of God's creative goals (including his goal to produce a world with significant freedom) to a greater extent than does this world. And this, these freewill theists adamantly maintain, is much less obvious. In fact, they contend, it is so dubious that (6) can be rejected.[31]

A third response is based on the alleged need for some unnecessary evil—evil that is not a necessary condition for some greater good—in a world containing individuals who are to make meaningful moral choices (or develop proper moral character). If God prevented all moral and/or natural evil that does not lead to a greater good within our world, it is argued, then it would not be possible for us to make significant moral decisions, since such decision-making requires our recognition of the fact that unnecessary evil can actually follow from our choices.[32] Likewise, if our world did not contain natural evils that lead to no greater good, we would not be in a position to develop a number of very positive human characteristics: courage, cooperation, compassion, patience.[33] Furthermore, these freewill theists continue, we have no way of knowing how much unnecessary evil is required in our world to achieve these ends. Hence to assume that a being with the properties of the God of BFWT would prevent more evil is unjustified.

In response to the moral challenge (the claim that a good God would not possess creative goals that require as much evil as we experience) freewill theists acknowledge that God could have actualized (could actualize) a world containing less horrific evil than exists in our world. They acknowledge, for instance, that God could have refrained from creating sentient creatures or could have created sentient creatures who only thought they were truly self-determining beings. However, freewill theists deny that a world of a different *type* than ours would in some obvious sense be morally preferable to the type of world we have. Those of a utilitarian persuasion believe that God is obligated to create that world which contains on balance the greatest net value, and they question whether a world containing no horrific evil but also no sentient creatures would possess greater net value than our world.

Moreover, many freewill theists of both utilitarian and deontological persuasion maintain that a world containing automata that only thought they were free would of necessity contain so much divine deception that the contention that such a world would be morally superior to a world containing truly free individuals does not possess even prima facie plausibility.[34]

Are these responses adequate? Do they meet the functional and moral challenges? Such responses are not, I believe, "explanations" for God's behavior that the critic must consider convincing. But the issue at hand is whether the *freewill theist* can justifiably deny (6)—that is, can justifiably deny the plausibility of assuming that the God of BFWT would allow less evil. And I see no reason why a freewill theist *cannot*, in response to the functional challenge, reasonably assume that we as humans are not in a position to determine with any degree of certainty exactly what ought or what ought not occur in a world controlled by an infinite creator or that the total causal nexus in our world is so complex and interrelated that we are simply not in a position to say with even prima facie plausibility that certain divine interventions would be on balance beneficial or that all of the evil we experience in this world is necessary to ensure the type of moral universe God desires. Nor do I see why a freewill theist cannot, in response to the moral challenge, justifiably affirm a model of divine goodness in relation to which a world such as ours is deemed superior to any other type of world in which less evil could be assured.

Consequently, I deny that a freewill theist must affirm (6).[35] And if a freewill theist need not grant the plausibility of assuming that a being with the acknowledged power, moral character and creative goals of the God of BFWT would do more to curtail evil, she can reject (10)—can justifiably deny that the evil in our world is incompatible with the existence of a being with the characteristics they attribute to their God.

But do most freewill theists deny (6)? There is an important

sense in which some clearly do not. Freewill theist C. Stephen
Evans, for instance, acknowledges that "the existence of evil *is* a
problem for the theist," one that "does 'count against' the existence
of God."[36] Moreover, for many other freewill theists, as well as
other theists, the staggering amount of horrific evil in our world
is not simply a theoretical issue to be discussed in a purely objective, academic manner. It is often troubling (even very troubling)
at an affective (existential or psychological) level. And it is difficult
to see why this would be so if it did not appear reasonable to these
theists, at least at times, that a being with the powers of the God
they worship could do more to prevent the evil we encounter.[37]

Let us assume for the sake of argument, accordingly, that (6) is
true and therefore that (7) must be affirmed (that we have prima
facie justification for believing that a world controlled by a being
with the properties of the God of BFWT would contain less horrific
evil). This brings us to a consideration of (8-10)—the question
whether the freewill theist can offer sufficient counterevidence.

The contention in (8), it should be explicitly noted, is not that a
person must in fact produce reasons for all of her beliefs. The claim,
rather, is only that if a person possesses some prima facie reason
for believing a proposition to be false, then she must sufficiently
counterbalance this "evidence" before she can maintain that this
proposition is true. And I find this principle to be perfectly reasonable.[38]

What, however, of (9)—the contention that no freewill theist can
justifiably maintain that there exist counterbalancing (sufficient,
equally plausible) reasons for rejecting the belief that a being with
the acknowledged power, moral character and creative goals of the
God of BFWT would not allow as much evil as we experience in
our world. This, as I see it, is the most important of the premises.
It is also the most ambiguous and thus needs initial clarification.
We are not in this context searching for actual reasons why a being
with the properties of the God of BFWT might allow as much evil

as we experience. That is, we are not searching for some specific explanation for the existence of so much seemingly unnecessary evil in a world allegedly controlled by the God of BFWT. Any "reason" of this sort would best be viewed as a basis for rejecting (6) (as a reason for denying that there is in fact a plausible basis for assuming that the God of BFWT would not allow as much evil as we experience).

The question at hand, rather, is the following: *If* freewill theists cannot explain why (i.e., furnish plausible reasons why) a being with the properties of the God of BFWT would allow so much evil, does there exist some *other basis* upon which they can successfully counter the claim that some of the evil in this world is in fact *excess* (is evil that a being with the acknowledged properties of the God of BFWT would not allow)?

Many freewill theists have thought so. And to help explain why, we will first consider a somewhat analogous human situation. Sue and Bill have been dating, and Bill has informed Sue that she is the only love in his life. However, while looking out her window later that night, Sue sees someone who appears to be Bill walking down the street with his arm around another woman, and thus finds herself wondering whether Bill was telling her the truth. What Sue would like at this point is an *unambiguous explanation:* an explanation that is subject to objective verification. She would like to discover, for example, that the young man was not really Bill or that the woman with whom he was walking was his sister who had arrived unexpectedly.

But what if it was Bill and he cannot offer an unambiguous explanation? What if the woman was Bill's former girlfriend, and he tells Sue that he was simply walking with her one last time to let her know that their relationship was finished and had his arm around her to soften the blow? That is, what if Bill offers an explanation that is not subject to objective verification? Or what if Bill offers no explanation at all? What if Bill tells Sue that he is not at liberty to offer an explanation or does not believe that he can offer one she will fully understand, and then asks her simply to believe that things are not as they seem—simply to believe that there is a sufficient reason for his behavior?

Would Sue be justified in continuing to believe that she is in fact Bill's only love? The answer, as I see it, depends on the nature of Sue's beliefs concerning Bill. If she has little reason to believe that Bill tells the truth in such contexts (if, for example, this is not the first time something like this has happened), then she may not be justified in believing Bill in this case. But what if Bill's moral character is beyond reproach? What if everyone agrees that Bill always tells the truth, and this always has been Sue's experience? The situation is then different. Most of us, I believe, would then appropriately acknowledge that she would be justified in continuing to believe that Bill loved only her, even if no clear explanation (or no explanation at all) were given.

Some freewill theists believe that a similar line of reasoning applies to the relationship between God and evil. They do not claim to be able to explain how each instance of evil in our world is either a necessary antecedent condition for, or an unavoidable byproduct of, the actualization of God's creative goals. Specifically, they do not claim to be able to demonstrate that God has beneficially withdrawn freedom or intervened in the natural order to the extent possible in every case. Nor do they deny that proponents of (9) can conceive of other types of worlds that the God of BFWT could have created (could create) that would *seemingly* contain less horrific evil. They acknowledge, rather, that the basis for their belief that this world does not in fact contain excess evil is solely (or primarily) because this is a logical consequent of their belief that the God of BFWT, who is perfectly good, exists and is the creator of this world.

However, they also contend that the evidence (grounds) for this belief—the various arguments for God's existence, their religious experiences, the reliability of their belief-forming faculties—can reasonably be held to outweigh the prima facie evidence against this belief produced by their inability to explain why the God of BFWT would not prohibit more of the evil we experience. And for this reason, these freewill theists believe they are justified in denying (9) (in denying that they can offer no counterbalancing evidence) and thus in denying (10) (in denying that they must acknowledge the reality of excess evil), even though they accept (6) (acknowledge that they cannot deny the plausibility of assuming that their God should do more).[39]

Is this a satisfactory response? Even some proponents of (6) think so. William Rowe, as noted, does not see how anyone can deny that it appears that a being with the acknowledged properties of the God of BFWT would prevent more evil. Moreover, he personally believes that there is no convincing argument for God's existence, and thus that he personally can deny rationally that the evil in our world is compatible with the existence of the God of BFWT. However, he does not deny that some theists have rational grounds for their theistic belief. And he acknowledges that those possessing such grounds can justifiably deny (9) (deny that they can produce no counterbalancing evidence) and thus that these theists can in principle also deny (10) (the reality of excess evil).[40]

Not all critics, however, are as charitable. Michael Martin is perfectly willing to grant that *if* the theist could offer positive evidence for God's existence that outweighed the prima facie evidence against God's existence generated by unexplainable evil, then rational theistic belief could be retained. However, he believes not only that "it is generally acknowledged even by many religious persons that the traditional arguments for the existence of God are bankrupt," but that "there is no positive evidence for belief in God that could outweigh the negative evidence." Accordingly, he concludes that the freewill theist cannot deny (10).[41]

But surely this will not do. Martin himself may be justified in believing that the traditional arguments are bankrupt, and perhaps he can find some theists who agree. But clearly it does not follow from any of this that no theist is justified in believing the traditional arguments to have some (or even considerable) strength. Moreover, even if a theist agrees that the traditional arguments are weak, Martin gives us no reason why this theist cannot maintain that one of the more contemporary arguments for God's existence (e.g., the cumulative case argument) has sufficient strength or why this theist cannot coherently maintain that her belief in God is properly basic—is justified apart from any propositional evidence of the traditional form. Consequently, I see no reason why any freewill theist is obligated to agree with Martin that "there is no positive evidence for belief in God that could outweigh the negative evidence," at least on the basis of anything he has said.[42]

Furthermore, I deny the existence of any set of neutral epistemic criteria that allow for the objective determination of whether a given body of "evidence" for belief in God outweighs a given body of "evidence" against this belief. It seems to me that Richard Swinburne is correct when he states that "everything turns on a quantitative moral judgement (i.e., a judgement about the *quantity* of evil which it is justifiable to bring about or to allow to occur, or the *quality* of good which it is obligatory to create)" and that "quantitative judgements are the hardest moral judgements on which to reach a sure conclusion."[43] In short, it seems to me that any such value judgment concerning God's existence must ultimately come down to a metaphysical "difference of opinion."[44] This in turn means that I deny that a freewill theist (or any other theist) must accept (9)—that is, I deny that a freewill theist cannot maintain that counterbalancing evidence for God's existence exists. Consequently, while I do not deny that the critic can maintain that the existence of the God of BFWT is incompatible with the evil we experience in our world, I do deny that any freewill theist must agree—that any freewill theist must affirm (10).

Conclusion

The purpose of this chapter has been to determine whether evil poses an insurmountable problem for the God of BFWT. The answer, I have argued, depends on whether freewill theists can maintain that this world contains no excess evil. Critics who deny that this is possible do not believe that freewill theists can offer a plausible reason why a being with the acknowledged power and character of the God of BFWT would allow as much evil as we experience, and furthermore possess no sufficient basis for retaining belief in the existence of the God of BFWT in the absence of such an explanation.

I have argued that while critics of BFWT can themselves reason in this fashion (and thus justifiably deny that the existence of the God of BFWT is compatible with the evil in our world), freewill theists can disagree. Freewill theists, I have argued, can deny the plausibility of assuming that a being with the properties of the God of BFWT would do more to rid the world of evil. And even if they can conceive of no plausible reason why God would not do more (and thus concede that evil counts against God's existence), the fact that freewill theists can justifiably affirm counterbalancing evidence allows them to maintain that this world in fact contains no excess evil and thus retain belief in the existence of God.

5
BASIC FREEWILL THEISM & PETITIONARY PRAYER

ALL MAJOR THEISTIC TRADITIONS EMPHASIZE THE IMPORTANCE of petitionary prayer—prayer in which God is asked to intervene beneficially in earthly affairs. The purpose of chapter five is to assess the relationship between basic freewill theism (BFWT) and this important theistic practice.

There are some senses in which proponents of all theistic perspectives can reasonably maintain that petitionary prayer is a meaningful, efficacious activity. First, all theists can justifiably maintain that petitionary prayer can beneficially affect the petitioner herself. For instance, all theists can consider prayers for safety to be efficacious in the sense that they make the petitioner more aware of potential danger. And no ones denies that prayers for others can promote increased sensitivity toward their needs and toward opportunities to help them. Second, all theists can maintain that petitionary prayer beneficially affects people who are aware that petitions are being offered on their behalf. All theists can maintain, for example, that the person in the hospital who knows that others are praying for him can benefit greatly from the knowledge that others are concerned about his welfare.[1]

However, many theists continue to believe firmly that whether God directly intervenes in our world depends at times on whether we use our power of choice to request such intervention. That is, many theists continue to believe that God has granted us the power to decide whether to request his assistance and that at times the decision we make determines whether we receive the help desired. Or, to state this important point differently, many theists continue to believe that at times we have not because we ask not, in the sense that certain states of affairs that God *can* and *would like* to bring about do not occur because *we* have chosen not to request that he intervene.

Theological determinists, however, cannot maintain that petitionary prayer is efficacious in this sense. They remain free to maintain that God has decided to bring about some states of affairs in response to requests that he do so and thus that petitionary prayer "changes things" in the sense that God may at times intervene in our world in ways that he would not have intervened if petitions had not been offered. For example, they can maintain that God touched a fevered body or guided the thinking of a world leader or granted peace to a troubled mind in ways that he would not have if petitions had not been offered.

But theological determinists maintain that God can unilaterally control voluntary human decision-making (that he can ensure that we always freely make the exact decisions that he would have us make).[2] Thus for theological determinists it can never be the case that God is prohibited from bringing about that which he can and would like to bring about (e.g., healing, guidance) because we have not requested that he do so. That is, it can never be the case that whether God brings about some state of affairs in our world depends on whether we utilize the power of choice granted us by God to petition his assistance.

As Thomas Aquinas clearly understood, for theological determinists "not only those things come about which God wills, but . . . they come about in the manner God wills them to. . . . The ultimate reason why some things happen contingently is not because their proximate causes are contingent, but because God has willed them to happen contingently, and therefore has prepared contingent causes for them."[3] In other words, if the God of theological determinism has decided to bring about some state of affairs in response to a prayer offered freely, he can *always* ensure that this prayer will be offered freely and thus that the desired state of affairs will come about. No person ever has it in his or her power to make it otherwise.

Process theists must also deny that petitionary prayer can ever be efficacious in the sense that it initiates unilateral divine activity that would not have occurred if it had not been freely requested.[4] Process theists believe that all entities—human and nonhuman, animate and inanimate—always possess some power of self-determination (freedom of choice). Hence, they must deny that God could ever unilaterally ensure any earthly outcome, whether asked to do so or not. Moreover, since process theists believe that God displays his concern for our world by presenting to every entity at every moment the best option available and then attempting to persuade each entity to act in accordance with it, they can never claim that petitionary prayer causes God to become more involved than he would otherwise have been. God is already involved in earthly affairs (e.g., in the sharing of wisdom or peace) to the extent that any petitioner could request that he be.[5]

For proponents of BFWT—hereafter referred to as freewill theists—the situation is quite different. Unlike theological determinists, freewill theists do *not* believe that God can unilaterally ensure that all and only that which he desires to come about will in fact occur in our world. They maintain, rather, that since God has chosen to create a world in which we possess significant freedom and since we can be significantly free only if he does not unilaterally control how this freedom is utilized, God voluntarily forfeits total control over earthly affairs in those cases where he allows us to exercise freedom of choice. Unlike proponents of process theism, freewill theists maintain that God does retain the power to intervene unilaterally in earthly affairs. Specifically, they believe that God retains the power to suspend freedom of choice and/or modify the natural order.[6] Consequently, proponents of BFWT are not limited to conceiving of petitionary efficacy in only those ways in which such efficacy can be affirmed by proponents of theological determinism and process theism. Like proponents of both of these other perspectives, freewill theists can maintain that prayer is efficacious in the sense that it can affect both petitioners and the objects of the petitions. And like proponents of theological determinism, freewill theists can maintain that petitionary prayer can be a component used by God to bring about desired ends.

It is also *possible*, though, for freewill theists to conceive of petitionary prayer as efficacious in a crucial sense that is not available to proponents of the other models. Since proponents of theological determinism believe that God always ensures that we freely make the exact decisions that he would have us make and since process theists deny that God can ever unilaterally intervene in earthly affairs, those in neither camp can maintain that petitionary prayer initiates unilateral divine activity that would not have taken place if we had not utilized our God-given power of choice to request such divine assistance. However, since proponents of BFWT deny that God can unilaterally control human decision-making that is truly voluntary but affirm that God can unilaterally intervene in earthly affairs, it becomes conceptually possible for freewill theists to maintain that petitionary prayer is efficacious in the sense in question—that is, to maintain that divine activity is at times dependent on our freely offered petitions. It becomes conceptually possible to maintain, for instance, that God guides a leader or soothes a troubled mind because we have utilized our God-given power of choice to request that he do so.

This does *not* mean, it is important to emphasize, that the God of BFWT necessarily possesses the ability to respond affirmatively to every request (or even to most requests) for assistance. As we saw in chapter one, while freewill theists do not deny that God has the capacity (power) to keep a person *in every case* from acting out her intentions and/or from having undesired consequences follow, freewill theists do deny that the God of BFWT could consistently and pervasively exercise his interventive powers in this manner.[7] Moreover, as we saw in the last chapter, the significance of this limitation is emphasized by freewill theists as a way to explain why God does not do more to rid the world of evil. Thus there may be some (perhaps even many) prayers for assistance that God would like to answer affirmatively but simply cannot. For instance, it is very unlikely that the God of BFWT could respond affirmatively to a request to keep all children safe from abuse, although God clearly has the power (and presumably the desire) to do so. But, given BFWT, it becomes conceptually possible to maintain that God does *on occasion* intervene in earthly affairs (e.g., on behalf of children) at least in part because his assistance was requested.[8]

Petitionary Prayer and God's Nature

Why would the God of BFWT require petitioning in those cases in which he *can* and would *like to* offer assistance? That is, in situations where the God of BFWT *can* intervene beneficially and *desires* to do so, why would he wait until requested to intervene? Why would he not intervene regardless of whether he has been asked to do so?

Michael J. Murray and Kurt Meyers have recently suggested that sometimes beneficial divine activity may be withheld until requested in order to help the believer learn more about God and thus become more like him.[9] Human parents, they point out, sometimes use the opportunity to respond to their children's petitions to "teach their children what is right and important and what is not." By refraining from granting certain requests (e.g., a sixteen-year-old son's request for a new red Corvette) "the parents indicate to the child that there are certain things that, for various reasons, are not in their interests, contrary to the child's belief." On the other hand, by granting certain requests, such as a child's request for help in making a gift for a sick neighbor, parents have "the opportunity to foster important virtues in the child."[10]

The same basic principle, they maintain, may also hold for the believer and his or her heavenly parent.

> The believer is not merely enjoined to pray for perceived needs, but to do so with the sort of humility that permits her to say "Thy will be done." If the request is granted, she not only has a need fulfilled, she has continued the process of learning what sorts of things are in accordance with God's will. Likewise, if the believer prays and her request is not granted, she learns that her desires are not in accordance with God's will.[11]

And by learning about God's will in this fashion, Murray and Meyers conclude, "the believer may in turn learn to become more righteous, and thus better conformed to the image of God."[12]

This suggestion has some initial plausibility. We would certainly not consider it unreasonable for a parent to require her children to ask for some of what she would like to give them primarily because she sees this as a means by which she can help her children identify consciously the values she would have them possess. Accordingly, it does not seem unreasonable in principle to assume that God might at times withhold provisions until requested because he believes (or knows) that our conscious consideration of his responses will help us learn more about his values (moral nature)[13] and thus become more like him.

However, my children can learn about my values through my responses to their requests *only if* they are *clearly* aware of the fact that I am the one who is giving (or withholding from) them that which they have requested and that my doing so is a good indication of my moral perspective toward that which they desire. Likewise, we can learn about God's values (his moral nature or general moral will) from that which occurs after we have made our petitions only to the extent that we can know with some degree of certainty that we are receiving (or not receiving) that which we have requested as a result of a decision made by God and that this decision was made *primarily* because our request was consistent (or inconsistent) with his values, that is, with how he would have us live.

However, as Murray and Meyers correctly note, it is always possible that a believer received his request not because God intervened directly in response but rather because the believer coincidentally requested something that was about to occur naturally anyway (in which case the request may not have been compatible with God's values). And they realize that incompatibility with divine values is not the only possible reason why a believer might not receive requested provision. Thus they acknowledge that a believer can never be *absolutely certain* on the basis of the "response" to any specific request that this petition "comports with God's will (or fails to)."[14] However, they do not view this as an insurmountable difficulty.

A week ago a colleague of ours sent a message to a philosopher she knew at another university. She asked whether or not he had written a paper on a certain subject and, if he had, whether he might send a copy of it. A few days later she received through the mail a copy of a paper on that very subject from that philosopher. It seems right to say that she is quite justified in believing that this paper was sent to her in light of the message she sent, even though it might well have been the case that this other philosopher had never received the message and had sent the paper simply believing that she might find it of interest. In the same way we suspect that believers are justified in holding that events that occur in accordance with petitions that they have made came about as a result of their prayer. As in the case of the paper, such beliefs are based on a sort of justification that is defensible. But the belief that the believer holds is nonetheless justified, and he would surely be epistemically permitted, if not obligated, to believe that the realization of the circumstances prayed for was an "answer" to his prayer . . . that God brought about (or failed to bring about) something that was petitioned for because He wanted things to come about in that way.[15]

This response strikes me as quite weak. First, let us consider cases in which theists do not receive their requests. Returning to our human analogy, let us assume that no paper is sent by philosopher A in response to the request from philosopher B. Let us further assume that a second request is sent by certified mail and that no paper (or response of any other type) is received. What exactly should philosopher B then conclude? Should she assume that philosopher A has the desired paper but simply does not want to send her a copy, or that philosopher A has the paper but has been too busy to send it, or that philosopher A does not have the paper and simply has not had the time or inclination to communicate this fact? All of these are possible explanations—that is, none can be defeated conclusively without further investigation. But in this case none of these possible explanations is obviously more plausible than the others. Therefore, it seems to me that it would be unreasonable for philosopher B to make assumptions about philosopher A's moral values or character on the basis of what has occurred (to assume, for instance, that he is uncaring or lazy) and even more unreasonable to act on these assumptions (to tell friends, for instance, not to expect a response from this fellow).

The same holds, I believe, with respect to requests made to God that go unfulfilled. Given any theistic perspective, it is *possible* that a petitioner has failed to receive a request because it was not in keeping with God's will—that is, was not consistent with God's values. But given any theistic perspective, an *equally plausible* alternative possibility always exists: although the request was perfectly compatible with God's moral nature, God decided for some other reason (e.g., for the overall good of the petitioner or someone else) not to grant the request (at least for now). Moreover, for freewill theists, God's decision to create a world in which individuals exercise meaningful freedom does in fact significantly (self-) limit his ability to intervene in earthly affairs. Thus another equally plausible possibility always exists: that the request was perfectly compatible with God's moral nature or values, but that God was not able to intervene in this case. Hence, I see no basis whatsoever for a theist, especially a freewill theist, to conclude solely or primarily on the basis of the fact that she did not receive her prayer request that the request itself was *most likely* not consistent with God's values.

But what of those cases in which a theist receives his or her request? Can it not be reasonable for a theist to assume that God was the source of the desired provision (and thus that the request was consistent with God's values)? It seems to me that the answer is clearly yes *if* we make an important assumption. We are clearly justified at the human level in believing that a person has responded affirmatively to a request if we *already* possess good reasons for believing that this person is likely to do so and there exists no equally plausible reason to think otherwise. For instance, to return to our test case, since philosopher B knows that most philosophers who receive requests for papers respond affirmatively and no equally plausible alternative explanation exists, she is clearly justified in believing that philosopher A sent the paper *in response to her request*. Likewise, it seems to me that *if* a believer who has received that which was requested in prayer already possesses a reasonable basis for believing that God answers prayers *of the type in question* affirmatively and she is aware of no plausible reason for believing either that God would not do so in her specific case or that the desired state of affairs was about to occur anyway, then she is perfectly justified in assuming that her prayer was answered by God.

That this is so, however, offers little help to Murray and Meyers in contending that God may at times refrain from granting a provision until petitioned so that the petitioner can learn something about his moral perspective (his values or moral nature). If a believer must have a reasonable basis for believing that God answers prayers of the relevant type *before* she can attribute any specific response to God, then she *already knows* that her request is compatible with God's moral nature. Therefore, the fact that her specific request has been granted can teach her nothing *new* about divine values. Or to rephrase this important point, a believer can learn something new about God's values or moral nature *as a result of an answer* to her prayer only if she is not certain when the petition is offered whether a request of this type is in keeping with God's general will. But if, as I maintain, one must already believe that such a request is compatible with God's values before one can conclude that any specific "response" is from God, then answered prayer can teach a believer nothing new about God's moral nature.

This is not to say that a believer can infer that God has responded affirmatively to a specific prayer only if she had beforehand a reasonable basis for assuming that God would do so *in this case*, that is, that God's specific will for her in this case is that she receive her request. As I see it, for instance, a believer could infer reasonably that God has responded affirmatively in specific instances (e.g., could come to believe that God has healed her mother or given her specific guidance) even though she had not been certain when making her requests that they would be granted. My argument is that if a believer has no prior basis for believing that requests of the type she is making are in keeping with God's moral nature, that is, for believing that the types of requests in question are in keeping with God's general will, then she is normally not in a position to maintain that an affirmative response has come from God.

Furthermore, it seems to me that most theistic traditions maintain at least implicitly that we are to use prayer to ask for only those things that we already believe are consistent with God's values in principle.

Accordingly, while I do not wish to claim that there could be no conceivable context in which a believer could maintain that she has learned something new about God's character (values, will) on the basis of the fact that she has received her request, I doubt that this could be the case normally. Thus I do not consider the suggestion that God at times withholds provisions until requested in order to help us learn divine values (and hence become more like God) to be a very plausible explanation for such divine behavior, especially for a proponent of BFWT.[16]

Petitionary Prayer and Divine-Human Relationships

Another possibility, which is in fact the most widely affirmed at present, is offered to us by Eleonore Stump.[17] God, she maintains, desires a loving, interactive relationship with us. But in any relationship between two individuals unequal in power and knowledge, she argues, it is possible for the more powerful to dominate or overwhelm the other in the sense that the more powerful imposes his or her will on the less powerful. For example, it is very possible for a teacher who sees a child at academic risk to impose her will on the child (e.g., to call the child's home or make the child stay after class) to the extent that she has infringed on the child's autonomy. Moreover, Stump continues, it is also possible for the less powerful person to become spoiled in the sense that she becomes dependent on the more powerful or simply takes for granted that which is given. A student, for instance, who is always automatically offered all available help by a teacher may come to assume that this is nothing less than what she deserves and thus may not appreciate the effort that the teacher is expending.[18]

The same, Stump argues, is true with respect to the relationship between God and us. Since God is so much more powerful and knowledgeable than we are, it would be quite easy for God to impose his will on us to the extent that we become simply slavish followers who lose "all sense of [our] own tastes and desires and will," or to furnish us with our needs to the point of spoiling us so that we come to depend upon or even expect God to do everything for us.[19]

But petitionary prayer, she maintains, can be a safeguard against these dangers. Just as a teacher might at times refrain from helping a student until asked in order to avoid dominating the student, it seems reasonable to assume that God at times refrains from giving us all he can and would like to give us until petitioned in order to preserve our autonomy as independent creatures. And just as parents sometimes refrain from giving their children all that they would like to give them so as not to spoil them, it seems reasonable to assume that God at times refrains from automatically giving us all that he can and would like to give us so that we do not become indulgent or fail to appreciate the source of that which we receive.

Stump's suggestion is initially attractive. It is certainly possible for the less powerful person in a relationship to become dominated or spoiled. Moreover, it seems reasonable to maintain that one way in which the more powerful person might counter these tendencies is for her not to do all she can and would like to do for the less powerful person until her assistance is requested.[20] Under closer scrutiny, however, two important questions arise. The first relates to intercessory prayer for others, which is one of the most important and common forms of petitionary prayer. While it might be reasonable to assume that a teacher would at times wait to help a needy student until such help was requested by this student in order to avoid dominating or spoiling him, is it reasonable to assume that a teacher who can and would like to help a student would refrain from doing so until such help was requested by a friend in order that the friend not be dominated or spoiled?

Likewise, while it may be reasonable to assume that God *at times* refrains from giving *a petitioner* something he can and would like to give *this person* until petitioned in order that *this person* not be spoiled or dominated, is it reasonable to assume that God would refrain from giving a person something that he can and would like to give this person until another person requests that he do so in order that the petitioner not be dominated or spoiled? For instance, while it might seem reasonable for God to refrain upon occasion from giving a person insight into a pressing problem until petitioned so as not to spoil or dominate this person, is it reasonable to assume that God would refrain from giving such insight to a person until requested to do so by another in order that the petitioner not be spoiled or dominated?[21]

My second question is related to the significance of those things requested from God. We can easily imagine a parent not buying a toy for a child or not allowing a child to watch TV or not taking a child to McDonalds until asked so that the child comes to recognize the source of these desired provisions. But can we imagine a parent justifiably refraining from having a child immunized or from giving a child enough food to develop properly or from shielding a child from abuse or from caring for the child's education needs until asked to do so by the child so that the child does not become dominated or spoiled? Or consider again the analogy of the needy student and concerned teacher. While it seems reasonable to assume that a teacher might not give a student all the extra tutorial help she could so as not to dominate him, is it reasonable to maintain that a teacher would allow a student to fail a course because she did not want to dominate or spoil him?

Likewise, we can divide those things that God can and would like to give us into those *basic provisions* that, if received, will keep our long-term quality of life (physical and mental well-being) from being diminished significantly and those *discretionary provisions* that, if received, will simply enhance our quality of life. For example, we can distinguish God's desire to protect a child from abuse (a basic provision) from his desire to help a family obtain financing for a new home (a discretionary provision).[22] And while it seems reasonable to assume that God might at times withhold discretionary provisions (the "little extras") to keep the believer from becoming spoiled or dominated, is it reasonable to assume that God would withhold basic provisions solely or primarily for the purpose of "relationship maintenance"? For instance, while it may be reasonable to assume that God will not help someone achieve the "American dream" until petitioned so as not to spoil her, is it reasonable to assume that God will not for this reason do all he can to protect the lives of innocent individuals until petitioned?

These questions are not unique to Stump's proposal. R. T. Allen contends that God refrains in some cases from giving us all he can until petitioned because of a desire to help us develop a concern for others:

> If we could not ask Him, in the straightforward sense which implies that we expect Him to do something and to do it because we ask, then the ways in which our moral concern could develop and express itself would be greatly restricted. . . . One can at least help through prayer to direct the divine activity . . . (because God does, on occasion, wait for us to ask Him). If this were not possible, one would be helpless to act, which may lead to indifference, for there would be no practical point in concerning oneself with such problems.[23]

Or consider Murray and Meyers's suggestion that God at times refrains from doing all he can and would like to do until petitioned because this "keeps the petitioner from a form of idolatry." When what a person desires comes to her as the result of her own human efforts, they point out, it is easy for this person to believe that she is the master of her own fate—to "worship" herself. But if God withholds what he would like a believer to receive at times until she asks for it, she is then forced "to consider that the goods that accrue to her do so ultimately because of forces beyond human control." That is, she is "forcefully reminded that she is directly dependent on God for her provisions in life . . . that God is the ultimate source of all goods."[24]

Or consider the contention that God refrains at times from doing all he can and would like to do until requested in order to reaffirm the faith of those who already acknowledge his existence or in order to display his existence to those who do not yet believe. With respect to each of these proposals, we encounter the same two basic moral tensions that arose with respect to Stump's proposal: Could a perfectly good God, for the reason in question, justifiably refrain from giving what he could and would like to give to *one person* until requested to do so by *another person?* And could a perfectly good God, for the reason in question, refrain from giving a person *basic provisions* (i.e., those things without which her long-term quality of life will be significantly diminished)? Accordingly, these questions must be given serious consideration.

The Ethics of Divine Response to Prayer

The correct answers to these questions, especially for proponents of BFWT, depend in part on the perceived moral basis for God's interaction with humans—the basis for divine ethical decision-making with respect to humans.[25] If a theist (of any sort) believes that *God is committed to doing all he can within the legitimate constraints inherent in this world to maximize the quality of life for each of us,* to conceive of God as withholding provisions until requested generates significant tensions. How could a God who can intervene and who desires the best for each individual refrain from doing something beneficial for one person primarily because to withhold such beneficial action will or could benefit another person? And how could a God who has an infinite amount of concern for an individual withhold from that individual something without which her long-term quality of life will be diminished significantly?[26]

What if a theist, however, denies that God must maximize the quality of life for each of us, maintaining instead only that *God must do all he can to ensure that each of our lives will be on the whole worth living?*[27] That is, what if a freewill theist, in agreement with Robert Adams, claims that a good God need only do all he can to ensure that "all of them would have satisfying lives on the whole."[28] Does it not then become more reasonable to maintain that God at times withholds something from one person for the sake of another or at times withholds even basic provisions from a person until requested?

In one sense the answer in both cases is yes. If God must ensure "only" that our lives will be on the whole worth living, then a decision by God to withhold something from one person primarily because it will benefit another person (e.g., increase her faith or reconfirm God's power or keep her from idolatry or from becoming spoiled) does, in principle, become less problematic. And it becomes less problematic to maintain that God at times withholds basic provisions from a petitioner.

As we saw in chapter three, however, a God who does not possess middle knowledge (MK) will not normally know all that a person will be experiencing. Thus unless a God without MK is committed to *unilateral* compensation in an afterlife when necessary,[29] he will not normally be in a position to know whether this person's existence, *without the beneficial intervention in question,* will in fact turn out on balance to be worth living. And if God does not have this knowledge, then it is questionable whether God could ever be (or at least could often be) in a position to do less than can be done for an individual, since to do so might bring it about (or at least increase the possibility) that this person's life will not on the whole be worth living. Moreover, even if we assume that God does possess MK, a difficulty concerning the withholding of basic provisions from a petitioner remains. By definition, to withhold a basic provision from a person is to withhold something necessary to keep this person's long-term quality of life from being diminished significantly. Hence it is not clear that God could, without *unilateral* compensation in an afterlife, normally ensure that a person's existence would be on the whole worth living if God even occasionally withheld *basic* provisions until they were requested.[30]

These tensions can, of course, be circumvented totally if it is held that God's only moral obligation with respect to sentient, self-determining beings is that he not allow any such being to suffer evil that he could prevent without negatively impacting his own creative goals.[31] It can then be argued that God can quite properly refrain from performing beneficial actions until requested, even when doing so proves very disadvantageous to some or many individuals, as long as his decision to do so contributes to that which God intends to bring about in our world, whether that be, for instance, his desire to display his power and glory, or his desire to create a world that on balance contains the greatest amount of value. However, freewill theists believe that God desires a world in which individuals practice meaningful moral autonomy. And if this is so, it is hard to understand how God could frequently use one individual as a "means" to a desired end for some other individual or how God could frequently withhold something important from an individual in order to bring about a desired end that is unrelated to this individual.

Accordingly, it is my overall assessment that while it is possible for a proponent of BFWT to maintain that God at times withholds that which he can and would like to give until petitioned, the standard explanations for such divine behavior offer little appeal for most proponents of BFWT.

Conclusion

What we have found is a somewhat paradoxical relationship between petitionary prayer and BFWT. Unlike theological determinists and process theists, proponents of BFWT can maintain that such prayer is, in principle, efficacious in the sense that God sometimes refrains from doing that which he can and would like to do until requested to do so. However, since proponents of BFWT believe that God's decision to create a world in which individuals exercise meaningful freedom does in fact significantly limit his ability to intervene in earthly affairs, it seems quite probable that there are many prayers for assistance that the God of BFWT would like to answer affirmatively but simply cannot.

Furthermore, most proponents of BFWT believe either that God must attempt to maximize the quality of life for each individual or that God is at least required to attempt to make the life of each individual on balance worth living. In either case, though, it becomes difficult to maintain that God would (or at least would often) withhold something from one person until requested to do so by another person primarily for the sake of the person making the request. And it becomes even more difficult to maintain that God would withhold basic provisions from a person—those things without which this person's life will suffer long-term negative effects—until such provisions were requested.

In short, while proponents of BFWT can maintain in principle that petitionary prayer changes things in the sense that our prayers initiate divine activity, the belief system of most also dictates, I believe, that the God of BFWT will actually refrain from doing what he can and would like to do until requested in a very limited number of cases.

Appendix
Simple Foreknowledge & Providential Control

In chapter two I argued that since there can never be a time at which a God who possesses complete simple foreknowledge (SFK) does not know all that will occur, and since foreknowledge can only be utilized in a providentially beneficial manner if there is a time at which what is foreknown can influence a divine decision that is not itself also already foreknown, there can exist no conceivable context in which SFK would enable God to make providentially beneficial decisions that he would not be able to make without this knowledge.

David P. Hunt believes that this difficulty can be circumvented by separating God's decision-making from his knowledge of the actual world.[1] Stated in my words, Hunt's argument runs as follows. Let us assume that before creation (and thus before God knew [logically speaking] what would occur in the actual world) God has formulated for every possible set of conditions, X, a conditional decision of the following type: *if X obtains, I will do Y because I desire to bring about Z.* Many of these conditionals describe what God will do at time $t2$ if X occurs at time t1. However, since God (per hypothesis) possesses foreknowledge in any world that he initiates, some of these conditionals describe what God will do at t1 if he *foresees* that X will occur at $t2$, producing the following form: if I know (possibly among other things) at time $t1$ that X will occur at time $t2$, then I will do Y at time $t1$ because I desire to bring about Z. What must be emphasized, though, even for conditional decisions of this type, is that no knowledge of the actual world was yet involved at the logical point in time at which God formulated such decisions. Only after his creative decision—only after he decided which actualizable world to initiate—did he see all that would actually occur in our world, including those antecedent conditions that would be actualized and thus see exactly what he would do in response.

However, if this is the basis for God's activity in our world, then the traditional problem with maintaining that God's foreknowledge can be of providential value (that by the time God has access to information about the future it is too late to be utilized in decision-making) no longer arises. Although it is still the case that God knows before doing anything in our world exactly what he will be doing and what will occur as a result, the decisions that are determining his actions were made before he had access to this information. Yet it can still be argued that foreknowledge gives God a providential edge, since those conditional decisions that include knowledge of future events in the antecedent conditions can still be said to trigger the implementation of efficacious divine activity that would otherwise not have occurred.

I am willing to grant that by placing the actual decision-making process prior to creation, the traditional problem with maintaining that SFK can give God a providential advantage can be circumvented. However, as I have argued in a previous essay, it appears to me that Hunt's "conditional decision" model is fatally flawed.[2] The best way to explain why this is so, I still believe, is to consider a specific scenario—for instance, Case 1, which was introduced in chapter two and is reproduced here.

Case 1. Tom has asked Sue to marry him, and she has prayed over his proposal. Among the beliefs that God holds as he considers Sue's prayer is the belief that Sue will respond negatively if her spouse dies a tragic death soon after marriage and thus that she ought not be encouraged to marry if it is known or believed that such a death will occur. Accordingly, because, and only because, God *foresees* that Tom is going to die in a horrible automobile accident a year from now, God attempts to influence Sue not to accept the proposal.

If we assume that God's attempt to convince Sue not to accept Tom's proposal is the implementation of a conditional decision made before creation, the crucial question for our purposes is, What exactly is the conditional decision that is triggering the divine activity in this case? Since what is allegedly initiating God's response to Sue is his *belief* that Sue ought not marry someone who will die soon after marriage and his *foreknowledge* of the fact that Tom is going to die in a year, it might appear that the relevant conditional in this case is the following:

(C1) I have decided (without knowing what will actually occur) that if Sue asks me whether she should marry Tom, and I believe that it will be best for Sue not to marry someone who will die tragically soon after their marriage, and I also know that Tom will die in an automobile accident a year from now, then I will attempt to convince Sue to reject Tom's proposal because I want what is best for Sue.

However, in any world, *W*, in which Sue asks God whether she should marry Tom and God foreknows that Tom will die tragically in a year, a God with *complete* foreknowledge also foreknows not only how he will respond to Sue's request in W but whether what is best for Sue will or will not come about. Thus *if* we assume that when God made his conditional decisions before creation he included in the antecedent conditions all the related information to which he would have access at the time they were implemented, then it appears that we must replace (C1) with some instantiation of the following conditional pattern:

(C2) I have decided (without knowing what will actually occur) that if Sue asks me whether she should marry Tom and I know that Tom will die in an automobile accident a year from now and *that I will attempt to convince Sue to reject Tom's proposal and that what is best for her will (or will not) come about*, then I will attempt to convince Sue to reject Tom's proposal because I want what is best for Sue.

But as Hunt himself has acknowledged in print, (C2) will not do. To say that God has decided to attempt to convince Sue to reject Tom's proposal under the conditions in question is to say that this decision is based in part on his knowledge of the fact that he will be making this decision. And, as Hunt correctly points out, "the fact that God *will* do A cannot be a reason for His deciding *to* do A."[3]

However, what if we assume, as Hunt does, that when formulating his conditional decisions, God was *not* required to take into consideration all the relevant data that would be available to him when these decisions were implemented? Specifically, what if we remove totally God's knowledge of how he is going to respond to Sue from the antecedent conditions and replace his knowledge of what is going to happen to Sue with a justified belief about what will quite probably come about if she refuses Tom's proposal. We are then left with the following variant of (C1):

(C3) I have decided (without knowing what will actually occur) that if Sue asks me whether she should marry Tom and I know that Tom will die in an automobile accident a year from now and I justifiably believe that if Sue refuses Tom's proposal it is quite probable that what is best for Sue will come about, then I will encourage Sue to reject Tom's proposal because I want what is best for Sue.

But could God in fact have consciously formulated conditionals such as (C3) before creation? That is, could he have formulated conditionals that did not include in the antecedent conditions his foreknowledge of what he will in fact do under these conditions and what will happen as a result? To answer this question, we must first consider the more general question of whether God could, before creation, have consciously formulated conditionals that do not contain in the antecedent conditions all the relevant data to which he would have access when these conditionals were implemented.

Of course it is not conceptually impossible to choose consciously not to consider all of the relevant data to which one has (or will have) access when making a decision. We humans often do so, perhaps because we fear that the consideration of such data will require us to make decisions that we do not want to make or because we simply do not have enough time to consider all the relevant data available or because we are simply too lazy to consider all the relevant data we could.

Unlike us, however, God is all-powerful and perfectly good. Thus the crucial question becomes, *Could God, as an all-powerful, perfectly good being,* have consciously formulated before creation conditionals (such as C3) that do not contain in the antecedent conditions all the relevant data to which he would have access at the time these conditionals were implemented? The answer to this question, it seems to me, is clearly no.

Even if God cannot be required to actualize the "best" option in each context (because the concept of a best option for God is incoherent),[4] he is, *as a perfectly good being,* at least committed to doing all he can in each context to actualize his creative goals (his desired ends). In any context, though, in which God purposely avoids the consideration of relevant data to which he has access, it is not only possible that he will make decisions that fail to actualize his desired ends to the extent they could have been actualized if he had considered all of the relevant data available, it is possible that his decisions will in fact significantly hinder the actualization of his creative goals. Thus if we assume that God is a perfectly good being, we must conclude, I believe, that he would *never* formulate conditional decisions before creation that did not contain in the antecedent conditions all the relevant data to which he would have access when these decisions were implemented.

But must God's foreknowledge of what he will actually do and what will actually follow as a result be considered "relevant data" in this context? It seems to me that the answer is clearly yes. For God to formulate conditional decisions such as (C3) before creation is for God to pledge that if the antecedent conditions ever hold in the actual world, then he will respond in the stipulated manner *regardless of what else he knows at that time*. It is possible, of course, that if God actualizes a world in which he sees (at the moment he initiates it) that the antecedent conditions in question hold, he might also at that moment see that the response to which he had obligated himself before creation does in fact produce the exact effect desired. With respect to (C3), for example, he might find that Sue does in fact refuse the proposal as the result of his urging and that she benefits as a result.

However, he might also see that the response to which he had committed himself before creation *does not* in fact bring about the desired results. He might, for instance, find to his dismay that the implementation of the consequent of (C3) is actually quite counterproductive in that it convinces Sue to make a decision that does not in fact lead to what is best for her. Hence since the very reason for the formulation of such conditionals is to help God maximize the actualization of his goals, I do not see how it can be denied that God's foreknowledge of what he will do in fact and what will follow in fact as a result is extremely "relevant data" in this context.

But if it is relevant data, then God, as a perfectly good being, must include this information in the antecedent conditions of any conditional decision he makes and hence cannot formulate conditional decisions such as (C3). He must formulate only totally inclusive conditionals such as (C2) instead. And by Hunt's own admission, the implementation of conditional decisions that include in the antecedent God's foreknowledge of what he is going to decide and what will occur as a result (the implementation of totally inclusive conditionals such as [C2]) cannot be providentially advantageous.[5]

Even if we assume for the sake of argument that I am wrong, that is, even if we assume that God could preclude what he will know about his actual behavior and its results from the antecedents of his conditional decisions, (C3) would still be inadequate. As I argued in my initial criticism of this conditional, even if we continue to grant that God's response to Sue's request could be triggered by antecedent conditions that do not include all that God would know about Tom and Sue at the time of this response, it still remains true that, in any world, W, in which Sue asks God at time t1 whether she should marry Tom, a God with SFK will know (among other things) at t1 in W whether Sue will refuse or will accept Tom's proposal and whether what is best for Sue will or will not come about as a result.

Let us assume first that what God knows in W is that Sue will *refuse* Tom's proposal and that what is best for her *will* come about as a result. In this case, God cannot believe in W that it is quite *probable* that what is best for Sue will come about if she refuses Tom's proposal. To believe that something will quite *probably* come about (as opposed to knowing with certainty that it will come about) is to acknowledge that it is *possible* that it might not come about. But if God *knows* in W that Sue will in fact refuse Tom's proposal and that it *will* in fact be best that she did, then God cannot simultaneously believe that it is even possible that what is best for Sue *might not* in fact come about in W if the proposal is refused.

An even more serious problem of this type arises if we assume that what God knows in W is that Sue will *refuse* Tom's proposal but that what is best for Sue *will not* in fact come about as a result. Not even God can believe that something is the case if he knows that it is not the case. Thus if God does in fact know in W that what is best for Sue will not in fact come about if she refuses Tom's proposal, then he cannot at the same time believe that it is quite probable that what is best for Sue will in fact come about if she refuses the proposal. And if God cannot hold this belief in W, then the antecedent conditions noted in (C3) can never be fully satisfied in W, and (C3) accordingly can never trigger providentially efficacious divine behavior in W.

Hunt finds this line of reasoning problematic on a number of counts. First, he challenges the manner in which I utilize the concept of probability in this context. "Of course," he acknowledges, "if probability is an ineluctably epistemic notion, it may not be possible to *believe* both" (1) that Sue refuses Tom's proposal and what is best for her does (or does not) in fact come about and (2) that if Sue refuses the proposal, what is best will probably come about. "But Basinger," he complains, "gives no reasons for adopting this interpretation of probability."[6]

I must confess that I do not know exactly what an "ineluctably [inevitably, unavoidably] epistemic notion of probability" is. But let me defend the relationship between probability and truth that I am presupposing in this context. It is true that if God at time t1 does not know what will actually occur if Sue refuses Tom's proposal, then God can at t1 believe that what is best for Sue will probably come about if she refuses Tom's proposal while also believing that what is best for Sue *either* will or will not in fact come about in this case.

However, as I am using the term *probability* in this context, to believe that something will quite probably come about (as distinct from knowing with certainty that it will come about) is acknowledging that it is possible that it might not come about. Given this relationship between probability and truth, if God actually knows at time *t1* that Sue will refuse Tom's proposal and what is best will (or will not) in fact come about, then God cannot at time *t1* also coherently believe that what he knows will occur may possibly not occur. Moreover, I am not familiar with any concept of probability that does allow for a person who actually knows that a given state of affairs will occur under conditions *C* to believe simultaneously that it is only probable (i.e., that it is less than certain) that this state of affairs will in fact occur under conditions *C*. At the very least, Hunt has not offered us one. So I stand by the concept of probability that I utilize.

It is Hunt's contention, however, that even if I can defend my notion of probability, to argue that God cannot believe simultaneously both that Sue will refuse Tom's proposal and that she might not do so is to step into a fatalistic trap.

> The usual "branching" view of the future, accepted by libertarians and (most) determinists alike, is that while a particular future *will* be actual, alternative futures are nevertheless (at least logically) *possible*. Now if this is true, why can't God believe it? Why can't God believe both that Sue refuses and prospers in the actual world and that she refuses and languishes in some merely possible world? Basinger seems to be saying that God cannot believe both of these things because they are *not* jointly true: if something *will* be the case, then it's not even *possible* that it *not* be the case. But then Basinger is a fatalist.[7]

Unfortunately, Hunt misunderstands that which I am claiming is not possible. My argument is not that it is impossible for God to believe that Sue in fact beneficially (or nonbeneficially) refuses Tom's proposal in the actual world and yet simultaneously believe that there are possible worlds in which she refuses with the opposite result. My argument rather is that it is impossible for God to know that Sue will in fact beneficially (or nonbeneficially) refuse Tom in a given world and yet believe simultaneously that she would only probably benefit (or not benefit) if she did so *in this same world*.[8]

There remains, however, another set of questions to be considered. What if God knows in W that Sue will *not refuse* Tom's proposal and that what is best for Sue *will* occur as a result? Or what if that which God knows in W is that Sue will *not refuse* Tom's proposal and that what is best *will not* occur as a result? In neither of these cases, I acknowledge, is God necessarily prohibited from affirming *counterfactually* that if Sue had refused Tom's proposal, it is quite probable that what is best for Sue would have come about. However, a belief about what would happen if Sue would reject Tom's proposal gives God absolutely no information about how Sue will (or even will probably) respond to Tom's death in a world in which *he knows* that she does *accept* Tom's proposal. And thus the implementation of (C3) in W under these conditions could in no sense make it more likely that what God desires to bring about, namely, that Sue respond to Tom's death in the best manner possible, will in fact come about in W *because of what God foreknows.* But this is exactly what *is* required for God's foreknowledge of Tom's death to be providentially useful.[9] So I stand by my original contention that the actualization of (C3), or any variant, cannot under any set of conceivable conditions trigger truly providentially efficacious divine activity.[10]

Hunt has one last complaint. As he sees it, "whatever difficulties" that my test case actually presents for his conditional model are a function primarily of the fact that in this scenario "God's purpose in acting as He does is achieved only if (i) His action leads to *something else* (beyond the action itself) and (ii) other agents are cooperative." In other scenarios (such as the following case, introduced in abridged form in chapter two) my objections to conditionals that preclude from the antecedent conditions what God knows he will do and what will occur as a result appear to Hunt "to be altogether inappropriate."[11]

Case 2. God wishes that the lost ark of the covenant not be found again until the Second Coming. *Foreseeing* that no one will ever look inside a particular cave in the side of a *wadi* not far from Jerusalem, He contrives to have the Ark slip from its litter and tumble into that very cave while a small band of Israelites spirits it away from their enemies under cover of darkness.[12]

But Hunt is incorrect on this point. Consider the relevant conditional related to this scenario:

(C4) I have decided (without knowing what will actually occur) that if a small band of Israelites is spiriting the ark of the covenant away from their enemies and I wish the ark of the covenant not to be found again until the Second Coming and I foresee that no one will ever look inside a particular cave, then I will contrive to have the ark slip from its litter and tumble into that very cave.

First, situations like this—situations in which God unilaterally manipulates the natural order in a certain manner *because* he foresees that such manipulation will bring about a desired end— are, in principle, dubious candidates to establish the efficacy of *foreknowledge*. If God is able to contrive to have the ark slip from its litter and tumble into that very cave, then there appears to be no reason why he cannot also contrive to ensure when necessary that no one will enter this cave until the Second Coming. And if he can do this, then he does not need foreknowledge to ensure his desired end. Present knowledge (PK) will do quite nicely.[13]

Even if this is not so—that is, even if the same end could not be ensured or at least could not be ensured as easily with PK alone— (C4) runs into exactly the same kinds of problems encountered in our discussion of (C1-C3) when considered in relation to a world in which God possesses complete foreknowledge. If God is perfectly good, then his desire in every world is always to actualize his providential goals. And if this is so, then God will wish for the ark not to be found in a given world *only if* God believes that this state of affairs will be providentially beneficial in that world. But if this is so and if God also has complete SFK in W (i.e., if God knows all that will ever occur in *W*), then he can wish that the ark not be found in W only if (1) he knows that it will be found but still believes it would have been beneficial had it not been found or (2) he knows that it is not found and that his goals were on balance benefited by this fact. But if his foreknowledge of this information is implicit in the antecedent of (C4), then (C4) (or any other conditional of its type)—again by Hunt's own admission—cannot be providentially beneficial for God, for we then again have God attempting to do something in part on the basis of the fact that he knows it will (or will not) come about. So I stand by my claim that SFK is of no greater providential value than PK alone.

Notes

Introduction

[1]See, for instance, David Ray Griffin, *God, Power and Evil: A Process Theodicy* (Philadelphia: Westminster Press, 1976), or J. L. Mackie, "Evil and Omnipotence," in *Philosophy of Religion: Selected Readings*, ed. William L. Rowe and William J. Wainwright, 2nd ed. (New York: Harcourt Brace Jovanovich, 1989), pp. 223-33.

[2]Among those who now explicitly acknowledge three categories are David Ray Griffin, *Evil Revisited: Responses and Reconsiderations* (Albany: State University of New York Press, 1991); Lewis S. Ford, "Divine Persuasion and Coercion," *Encounter* 47, no. 3 (Summer 1986): 267-74; William Hasker, *God, Time and Knowledge* (Ithaca, N.Y.: Cornell University Press, 1989); John Feinberg, *The Many Faces of Evil* (Grand Rapids, Mich.: Zondervan, 1994).

[3]The leading contemporary proponents of process thought are David Ray Griffin, Lewis S. Ford (*The Lure of God* [Philadelphia: Fortress, 1978]) and John B. Cobb Jr. (*God and the World* [Philadelphia: Westminster Press, 1969]). See chapter one, pp. 22-23, for a fuller discussion of this theological perspective.

[4]Contemporary proponents of theological determinism include Gordon Clark, *Religion, Reason and Revelation* (Philadelphia: Presbyterian & Reformed, 1961), and Gerrit C. Berkouwer, *The Providence of God* (Grand Rapids, Mich.: Eerdmans, 1952). Historically, Luther and Calvin clearly fit into this category. See chapter one, pp. 27-29, for a fuller discussion of theological system.

[5]I believe that I am the first person to have used the phrase "freewill theism" *in this exact manner.* See my "Human Freedom and Divine Providence: Some

Others who now do so include Hasker in *God, Time and Knowledge* and Griffin in *Evil Revisited*. A list of those I believe to be freewill theists can be found in chapter one, note 28.

[6]This does not mean, as we shall see, that freewill theists deny that God can influence voluntary decision-making, especially in those cases where an individual is open to God's leading. What is denied, rather, is that God can grant an individual freedom of choice and yet *ensure* that this person will make the decisions God would have her make.

[7]All freewill theists with whom I am familiar are ontological realists in the sense that they believe the reality about which they are theorizing to be independent of their attempts to understand it. But some, such as John Hick, are Kantian in their epistemology. While they too maintain that their beliefs are about an independent reality, they deny that we as humans have direct access to this reality and thus maintain that our beliefs are about this reality *as it appears to us*. See, for instance, John Hick, "Religious Pluralism and Salvation," *Faith and Philosophy* 5, no. 4 (October 1988): 365-77, and his *God Has Many Names* (London: Macmillan, 1980).

Furthermore, to say that freewill theists who hold beliefs about an independent reality are ontological realists leaves open the question of exactly how the language that expresses these beliefs is to be understood. All will agree that some such expressions—for instance, "God speaks to us"—must be understood analogically as opposed to univocally or equivocally. But freewill theists often differ on the extent to which these analogies hold.

[8]In one sense, of course, epistemological assessment incorporates ontological assessment. Given most models of justified belief, if we can establish that the world is not the way someone believes it to be, then the belief in question cannot, in principle, be affirmed justifiably. But even if we cannot determine whether a belief is true, we can still ask whether the affirmation of this belief is justified. And thus epistemological assessment must be distinguished at least conceptually from its ontological counterpart.

[9]Unfortunately, there exists no comprehensive set of necessary and sufficient conditions for justified belief accepted by all (or most) philosophers. Nor do I believe that it is possible to argue in an objective, straightforward manner for the clear superiority of any set of such conditions. Thus I do not believe it will be possible to assess the belief system of freewill theists in a manner *totally* free of significant epistemic ambiguity.

However, the vast majority of philosophers (including almost all freewill theists and their critics) agree that at the very least a set of beliefs can be affirmed justifiably only if this set does not contain beliefs that are false, incoherent (meaningless or self-contradictory) or incompossible (cannot be affirmed simultaneously). Moreover, every relevant epistemic challenge to FWT with which I am familiar is based on the claim that the affirmation of some belief or set of beliefs is unjustified because it is in fact false or self-contradictory or incompossible with other beliefs. Accordingly, these are the criteria for justified belief on which my assessment of FWT will be based. For a more detailed discussion of my perspective on this issue, see my "The Rationality of Belief in God: Some Clarifications," *New Scholasticism* 60, no. 2 (Spring 1986): 163-85.

[10]I believe that I am the first person to have used "present knowledge" to characterize this model of divine omniscience ("Middle Knowledge and Classical Christian Thought," *Religious Studies* 22 [1986]: 407-22). The most common label for this form of divine knowledge remains "limited omniscience." See, for instance, Francis J. Beckwith, "Limited Omniscience and the Test for a Prophet: A Brief Philosophical Analysis," *Journal of the Evangelical Theological Society* 36, no. 3 (September 1993): 357-62. It is my opinion, however, that such a descriptor begs the question.

[11]The leading proponent of this perspective is Alvin Plantinga. See his "The Foundations of Theism: A Reply," *Faith and Philosophy* 3, no. 3 (1986): 298-313. Other influential philosophers of religion, such as Thomas V. Morris, also seem to fit into this category, at least at times. See, for example, Morris's *Anselmian Explorations: Essays in Philosophical Theology* (Notre Dame, Ind.: University of Notre Dame Press, 1987).

[12]It is only fair to note that a significant number of theists (and nontheists) are not as "pessimistic" at this point. Many believe that it can be demonstrated conclusively (or at least with reasonable certainty) that their theistic (or nontheistic) perspective is superior to competing worldviews. Theists in this category include Griffin, *Evil Revisited;* Norman Geisler, "God Knows All Things," in *Predestination and Free Will*, ed. David and Randall Basinger (Downers Grove, Ill.: InterVarsity Press, 1986), pp. 63-84; and Brad Stetson, *Pluralism and Particularity in Religious Belief* (Westport, Conn.: Praeger, 1994). Nontheists in this category include Antony Flew, *The Presumption of Atheism* (London: Pemberton, 1976), and J. L. Mackie, *The Miracle of Theism* (Oxford: Clarendon, 1982).

[13]Again, it is important to note that neither I nor proponents of bunker theology deny the existence of some objective criteria for the assessment of worldviews, for instance consistency and comprehensiveness. But we do deny that such criteria are even in principle sufficient to decide the issue in favor of any one perspective.

[14]An expanded version of this critique of "bunker theology" appears in my "Plantinga, Pluralism and Justified Religious Belief," *Faith and Philosophy* 8, no. 1 (January 1991): 67-80. Also see my "Pluralism and Justified Religious Belief: A Response to Gellman," forthcoming in *Faith and Philosophy*.

Chapter 1: Basic Freewill Theism
[1]The most persuasive philosophical pantheist, I believe, remains Spinoza.

One of the most influential deists is Thomas Paine. The best-known proponent of finitism is probably Edgar S. Brightman.

[2]As stated in the introduction, the term "freewill theism" is used in this book to refer to a specific theological perspective on the relationship between God and the world. Thus while I believe there are in fact many theists who affirm this perspective (and will later in this chapter identify some), my primary intent is not to argue whether any specific theist does or does not fit into this category.

[3]William Rowe, "Ruminations About Evil," *Philosophical Perspectives* 5 (1991): 79.

[4]David Ray Griffin, *Evil Revisited: Responses and Reconsiderations* (Albany: State University of New York Press, 1991), p. 23.

[5]Ibid., p. 26.

[6]This illustration was generated by Randall Basinger.

[7]The basic metaphysical roots of process theism are found in the work of Alfred North Whitehead (1861-1947). Much of its explicit theological framework was the result of the interpretation of Whitehead offered by Charles Hartshorne. Leading contemporary proponents include Lewis S. Ford, David Griffin and John B. Cobb Jr. The best introductory discussion of process thought remains Cobb and Griffin, *Process Theology: An Introductory Exposition* (Philadelphia: Westminster Press, 1976). The most rigorous defense of process thought is Griffin's *Evil Revisited*. I offer a challenge to the self-consistency of process thought in *Divine Power and Process Theism: A Philosophical Critique* (Albany: State University of New York Press, 1988).

[8]The most famous proponent of this view, often labeled "absolute omnipotence," was Descartes, who saw the affirmation of this perspective essential to preserving God's sovereignty. Melville Y. Stewart offers a useful discussion of Descartes's position in *The Greater-Good Defense* (New York: St. Martin's, 1993), pp. 21-25.

[9]Thomas V. Morris, *Our Idea of God* (Downers Grove, Ill.: InterVarsity Press, 1991), p. 66. C. S. Lewis makes the same point in *The Problem of Pain* (New York: Macmillan, 1962).

[10]Even this definition is problematic, but it will serve our present purposes adequately. For three useful but distinct discussions of the concept of omnipotence, see Morris, *Our Idea of God*, chap. 4; Edward R. Wierenga, *The Nature of God: An Inquiry into Divine Attributes* (Ithaca, N.Y.: Cornell University Press, 1989), chap. 1; and Stewart, *Greater-Good Defense*, pp. 21-32.

[11]As we shall soon see, a number of classical theists believe that God can bring about states of affairs that will always *appear to us* to be logically impossible, even though they *really* are not.

[12]The line between that which is impossible and that which is not compossible is not an absolute one. It might be argued, for example, that since the existence of a circle is possible and the existence of a square is possible, the

existence of a square circle is best thought of as something not compossible. Or it might be argued that for a person to be both twenty-five years old and dead at the same time is simply an impossibility. But since the distinction in question is a common one and does not affect the outcome of anything else I argue, I have elected to acknowledge it.

[13]This is not to say that many theists have not seen God's inability to bring about that which is logically impossible as *important*. Leïbniz, for example, sees it as one reason for the existence of evil in our world. But even he does not assume that this is a limitation that God wishes he could at times circumvent.

[14]Some classical theists believe that certain personal, conscious nonhuman causal agents (e.g., angels and demons) also have the capacity to choose and act voluntarily.

[15]While most classical theists agree that lack of coercion is a necessary condition for free choice, many do not consider it sufficient. For instance, some maintain in true Aristotelian fashion that an act is voluntary for a person only if this person is the sole cause of the state of affairs in question.

[16]*Compatibilism* is used in its most popular sense: as a label for the contention that causal determinism is compatible with human freedom. I am, though, restricting my present discussion to the compatibility of determinism with human *choice*, since to expand the discussion to include the compatibility of determinism with human *activity* raises issues (e.g., "Frankfurt-type" counterexamples) that are not relevant at this point. See Wierenga, *Nature of God*, pp. 74-85, for a good discussion of the problems that arise when compatibilism is considered primarily in terms of human activity—that is, in terms of our responses to our choices. Ted Honderich offers a very helpful discussion of the thorny issues surrounding the general compatibilism-incompatibilism debate in *How Free Are You?* (New York: Oxford University Press, 1993), chap. 8.

[17]Honderich, *How Free Are You?* chap. 8.

[18]See, for example, Gordon Clark, *Religion, Reason and Revelation* (Philadelphia: Presbyterian & Reformed, 1961), and Gerrit O. Berkouwer, *The Providence of God* (Grand Rapids, Mich.: Eerdmans, 1952). Luther and Calvin are clearly theological determinists. And occasionally Thomas Aquinas appears to fit into this category. For example, at one point when discussing the relationship between human freedom and divine control, Aquinas states that "not only those things come about which God wills, but they . . . come about in the manner that God wills them to. . . . The ultimate reason why some things happen contingently is not because their proximate causes are contingent, but because God has willed them to happen contingently, and therefore has prepared contingent causes for them" (*Summa Theologiae* 1a.19.8). But it is not clear to me, given all of his relevant comments, that Aquinas is best considered a theological determinist.

[19]R. B. Kuiper in *The Voice of Authority*, ed. G. W. Marston (Philadelphia: Presbyterian and Reformed, 1960), p. 16.

[20]J. I. Packer, *Evangelism and the Sovereignty of God* (Chicago: Inter-Varsity Press, 1961), p. 24.

[21]Ibid., p. 23. For an expanded discussion of this perspective, see my "Biblical Paradox: Does Revelation Challenge Logic?" *Journal of the Evangelical Theological Society* 30, no. 2 (June 1987): 205-13.

[22]It is my belief that Augustine is clearly a theological determinist. He states at one point, for example, that "God is called Almighty for no other reason than that he can do whatever he willeth and because the efficacy of his omnipotent will is not impeded by the will of any creature" (*Enchiridion* 14.96). But I am not certain whether he is best viewed as a compatibilist or an incompatibilist.

[23]The leading proponent of this perspective is John Feinberg. See Feinberg, *The Many Faces of Evil* (Grand Rapids, Mich.: Zondervan, 1994), chap. 6. Martin Davies also defends this perspective, although it is not clear whether he is actually a proponent of this position. See Davies, "Determinism and Evil," *Australasian Journal of Philosophy* 58, no. 2 (June 1980): 116-27.

[24]Davies, "Determinism," p. 119.

[25]Feinberg, *Many Faces of Evil*, p. 130.

[26]Davies, "Determinism," p. 124.

[27]Feinberg, *Many Faces of Evil*, p. 130.

[28]As stated earlier, I am interested in discussing a theological position, not in attempting to determine with exact specificity whether given individuals do in fact belong in this category. But the following are clearly freewill theists: Richard Swinburne, *The Coherence of Theism* (Oxford: Clarendon, 1977), *The Existence of God* (Oxford: Clarendon, 1979), *Responsibility and Atonement* (Oxford: Clarendon, 1989); John Hick, *Evil and the God of Love* (London: Macmillan, 1966); William Hasker, *God, Time and Knowledge* (Ithaca, N.Y.: Cornell University Press, 1989); Michael Peterson, *Evil and the Christian God* (Grand Rapids, Mich.: Baker Book House, 1982); Bruce Reichenbach, *Evil and a Good God* (New York: Fordham University Press, 1982).

I also believe that Alvin Plantinga, William Alston, George Mavrodes and Edward Wierenga probably fit into this category.

[29]Reichenbach, *Evil and a Good God*, p. 60.

[30]The claim here, it must be reemphasized, is not that God cannot attempt to influence free choice or that his influence cannot be efficacious. The claim, rather, is that such influence cannot be compelling. If a decision is truly free, then the person making the choice can choose not to act as God would have her act.

[31]See, for example, Alvin Plantinga, *God, Freedom and Evil* (Grand Rapids, Mich.: Eerdmans, 1977), p. 30.

[32]Variations of this argument appear, for instance, in Reichenbach, *Evil and a Good God*, chap. 5; Peterson, *Evil and the Christian God*, chap. 5; and Swinburne, *Existence of God*, chaps. 10-11.

[33]For an extended dialogue on this question, see David Basinger and Randall Basinger, "Divine Omnipotence: Plantinga vs. Griffin," *Process Studies* 11, no. 1 (Spring 1981): 18; Griffin, *Evil Revisited*, pp. 18, 83-87; David Basinger, "Process Theism Versus Free-Will Theism: A Response to Griffin," *Process Studies* 20, no. 4 (Winter 1991): 209-10.

[34]Variations of this line of reasoning appear, at least implicitly, in Hick, *Evil and the God of Love*; Peterson, *Evil and the Christian God*, chap. 5; and Swinburne, *Existence of God*, chaps. 10-11.

[35]Hick, *Evil and the God of Love*, pp. 307-13.

[36]Hasker, *God, Time and Knowledge*, p. 196.

[37]Stewart, *Greater-Good Defense*, p. 50.

[38]Enough has already been said, obviously, to allow for at least one legitimate epistemic challenge to BFWT. As we have seen, all freewill theists maintain that God has created a world in which individuals possess libertarian freedom—that is, maintain that indeterminism holds in the realm of human decision-making. Thus if determinism holds (i.e., if all human activity, including all choice, is the result of conditions such that, given these conditions, no other choice could have been made), BFWT must be rejected. I do not believe, however, that either determinists or indeterminists have yet established in an objective, nonquestion-begging manner that the opposing perspective is false. (Again, see Honderich, *How Free Are You?*) Hence I believe personally that the consideration of this question does not automatically rule out BFWT.

I acknowledge that some determinists will not agree with me on this point; they see the issue as settled. And I do not have any response that has not already been offered many times before. Accordingly, I shall simply assume for the remainder of our discussion that indeterminism can be affirmed. Those determinists who believe otherwise are still invited, though, to consider hypothetically whether BFWT could be affirmed (or what proponents of BFWT could affirm) if indeterminism were true.

[39]Sometimes it is incorrectly stated or implied that a given freewill theist's perspective on one of these issues is a basic tenet of FWT. For example, David Griffin wrongly implies that all freewill theists maintain that God's primary purpose in creating a world such as ours was his desire for soul-making. See *Evil Revisited*, pp. 18-19, and my response in "Process Theism Versus Free-Will Theism," pp. 208-9.

[40]To focus primarily on the logical coherence (and implications) of BFWT is, I grant, a limited goal. However, I see this exercise as an essential starting point in any serious consideration of this (or any other) theological perspective.

Chapter 2: Basic Freewill Theism & Divine Omniscience

[1]See chapter one, pp. 32-36.

[2]A God with PK may, however, have a very good idea of who will probably be elected.

[3]It is important to add parenthetically that timeless knowledge also normally fits into this category. The proponent of timeless knowledge usually maintains that God's knowledge of all actual occurrences (those that from our perspective are past, present or future) is not "in time." All occurrences are being viewed by God in the "eternal now." This differs from simple foreknowledge in that God is not said to foreknow anything. But it is similar in that both models maintain that God knows all that was, is or will be actual from our perspective. For an excellent discussion of the concept of timeless knowledge, see William Hasker, *God, Time and Knowledge* (Ithaca, N.Y.: Cornell University Press, 1989), chaps. 8-9.

[4]Proponents of timeless knowledge could in principle also affirm a version of middle knowledge, although I am not aware of any who do. For example, it could be claimed that in addition to "timelessly" seeing the actual world in its entirety, God not only timelessly "sees" all other possible worlds in their entirety, but can also identify which of these worlds would have been actual, given that other creative decisions had been made.

[5]Alvin Plantinga, *The Nature of Necessity* (Oxford: Clarendon, 1974), p. 180. This characterization of the three forms of divine omniscience is a slightly varied version of what first appeared in my "Middle Knowledge and Classical Christian Thought," *Religious Studies*, 1986, pp. 407-8.

[6]See, for example, William Hasker, "Providence and Evil: Three Theories," *Religious Studies* 28 (1992): 91-105.

[7]Again, this characterization of the three models of divine omniscience is a slightly modified version of what first appeared in my "Middle Knowledge and Classical Christian Thought," pp. 407-8.

[8]An influential theological critic of the possibility of SFK is Clark Pinnock. See, for example, "God Limits His Knowledge," in *Predestination and Free Will,* ed. David and Randall Basinger (Downers Grove, Ill.: InterVarsity Press, 1986), pp. 143-62. Two influential critics of the possibility of MK are Robert Adams and William Hasker. See, for example, Adams, "Middle Knowledge and the Problem of Evil," *American Philosophical Quarterly* 14, no. 2 (1977): 109-17; Hasker, "A Refutation of Middle Knowledge," *Nous* 20 (1986): 545-57.

[9]My defense of the possibility of MK appears in "Middle Knowledge and Human Freedom: Some Clarifications," *Faith and Philosophy* 4, no. 3 (1987): 330-36. Others who defend the possibility of MK are Edward Wierenga, *The Nature of God* (Ithaca, N.Y.: Cornell University Press, 1989), chap. 5; Thomas Flint, "Hasker's *God, Time and Knowledge,*" *Philosophical Studies* 60 (1990): 103-15; Richard Otte, "A Defense of Middle Knowledge," *International Jour-*

nal for the Philosophy of Religion 21 (1987): 161-69. Wierenga also defends the possibility of SFK in *Nature of God*, chap. 2.

[10]Three of the most comprehensive discussions of this issue are found in Wierenga, *Nature of God*, chaps. 3-4; Hasker, *God, Time and Knowledge*, chaps. 1-7; and William L. Craig, *Divine Omniscience and Human Freedom* (Leiden: E. J. Brill, 1990).

[11]William Craig, *The Only Wise God* (Grand Rapids, Mich.: Baker Book House, 1987), p. 135.

[12]Ibid.

[13]This criticism of Craig's position first appeared in my "Divine Control and Human Freedom: Is Middle Knowledge the Answer?" *Journal of the Evangelical Theological Society* 36, no. 1 (1993): 60-63.

[14]Hasker, *God, Time and Knowledge*, p. 198.

[15]A version of my critique of Hasker first appeared in "Middle Knowledge and Divine Control," *International Journal for Philosophy of Religion* 30 (1991): 135.

[16]Francis J. Beckwith, "Limited Omniscience and the Test for a Prophet: A Brief Philosophical Analysis," *Journal of the Evangelical Theological Society* 36, no. 3 (September 1993): 357-62.

[17]Ibid., p. 359.

[18]Some qualification is necessary, since it is simply not true that there is no possible world in which what a prophet of God says will occur does not in fact occur. For instance, in Amos 7:1-6 and Isaiah 38:1-5, prophets speaking for God make predictions that do not in fact come to pass (as God in each case relents). But most Christians with a high view of Scripture (including most freewill theists with a high view of Scripture) will grant that when a spokesperson for God is actually stating what God will in fact do, this person cannot be wrong.

[19]My discussion of Beckwith's challenge is an abridged version of what first appeared in "Can an Evangelical Christian Justifiably Deny God's Knowledge of the Future?" *Christian Scholar's Review* 25, no. 2 (December 1995): 113-45.

[20]This is an abridged version of a scenario created by David P. Hunt, "Prescience and Providence: A Reply to My Critics," *Faith and Philosophy* 10, no. 3 (July 1993): 437.

[21]I have given what I see as the strongest argument against the providential efficacy of SFK. The same conclusion can be reached in a number of other ways. For example, see Hasker, *God, Time and Knowledge*, chap. 3, or my "Middle Knowledge and Classical Christian Thought," pp. 413-20.

Some proponents of SFK (for instance, Duns Scotus) argue that God's knowledge has a logical (nontemporal) order and thus that a God with SFK can, in a certain logical sense, know what will occur before it does. However, this distinction is of no value in this context. It may well make sense to say that a God with SFK did not know before his creative decision (in some logical, nontemporal sense) which possible world would in fact be actual. But following his creative choice, a God with SFK saw instantaneously all that would ever occur in its entirety. Thus since SFK can be efficacious in our world (in the world God chose to create) only if there is a time in our world at which God does not yet know what he will decide to do, SFK cannot be of providential value.

[22]David P. Hunt believes that this difficulty can be circumvented by separating God's decision-making from his knowledge of the actual world. His argument and my response are quite technical and thus have been relegated (for the philosophically hardy) to the appendix following chapter five.

[23]See David Basinger, "Practical Implications," in Clark Pinnock et al., *The Openness of God: A Biblical Challenge to the Traditional Understanding of God* (Downers Grove, Ill.: InterVarsity Press, 1994), pp. 155-76, for a discussion of my own position on this question.

Chapter 3: Basic Freewill Theism & God's Moral Nature (Goodness)

[1]See Thomas V. Morris, *Our Idea of God: An Introduction to Philosophical Theology* (Downers Grove, Ill.: InterVarsity Press, 1991), chap. 3.

[2]Ibid., p. 51.

[3]For Leibnizians and other theological determinists, "best *actualizable* world" is synonymous with "best *possible* world," since all possible worlds are for them actualizable. However, as we have seen in previous chapters, this is not the case for freewill theists, who deny that all possible worlds containing free creatures are actualizable.

[4]Proponents of (P2) include Robert Elliot, "Divine Perfection, Axiology and the No Best Worlds Defence," *Religious Studies* 29 (December 1993): 533-42, and Morris, *Our Idea of God*, chap. 8. Proponents of (P3) include Peter Forrest, "The Problem of Evil: Two Neglected Defenses," *Sophia* 29 (1981): 52-54, and John D. McHarry, "A Theodicy," *Analysis* 38 (1978): 132-34.

[5]See, for example, George Schlesinger, *Religion and the Scientific Method* (Dordrecht, Netherlands: Reidel, 1977), pp. 59-80; Bruce Reichenbach, "Must God Create the Best Possible World?" *International Philosophical Quarterly*, June 1979, pp. 203-12; Forrest, "Problem of Evil," pp. 52-54; McHarry, "Theodicy," pp. 132-34; William Mann, "The Best of All Possible Worlds," in *Being and Goodness: The Concept of Good in Metaphysics and Philosophical Theology*, ed. Scott MacDonald (Ithaca, N.Y.: Cornell University Press, 1991), pp. 250-77.

[6]David Basinger, "Divine Omniscience and the Best of All Possible Worlds," *Journal of Value Inquiry* 16 (1982): 143-48.

[7]One of the (very helpful) reviewers of this manuscript believes that whether God can know the net value in any possible world is the very issue to be decided and thus I am at this point simply begging the question. This

criticism, however, seems to be based on a confusion. As I understand it, those who claim that God cannot identify a best possible world do not do so because they believe that *within* any given possible world there could always be more value. (Any given possible world with something added is in fact a different possible world.) Their argument is that the set of actualizable worlds is infinite—that is, that for each world God could create, another world could be created. Thus while to claim that God can know the net value in each possible world is, I grant, debatable, it is not question-begging.

[8]Aquinas, for one, was quite willing to make such an admission. "Since God knows not only things which actually exist but also those which can be produced either by himself or by creatures, as we have shown, and it is established that these are infinite in number, we must hold that God knows infinites. . . . A thing is said to be known comprehensively when no part of it remains beyond the knower's grasp. Therefore, it is not contrary to the notion of an infinite that it should be known comprehensively by the infinite" (*Summa Theologiae* 1a.14.12; ed. Thomas Gilbey [Garden City, N.Y.: Image/Doubleday, 1969]).

Aquinas, however, denies that there exists a best actualizable world. For a helpful discussion of his position, see Evan M. Fales, "Divine Freedom and the Choice of a World," *International Journal for the Philosophy of Religion* 35 (1994): 69-73.

[9]Exactly what it means for a being's quality of life to be "maximized" will, of course, differ (possibly quite significantly) from moral theory to moral theory. The claim here is only that God, as a perfectly good being, must do everything possible to ensure for each of us that our quality of life (however this is interpreted) is as high as possible.

[10]Versions of (M1) are affirmed by Keith Yandell, "The Greater Good Defense," *Sophia* 13, no. 3 (October 1974): 1-16, and Melville Stewart, "On Felix Culpa, Redemption and the Greater Good Defense," *Sophia* 25, no. 3 (October 1986): 18.

[11]Fyodor Dostoyevsky, *The Brothers Karamazov*, trans. David Magarshack (Baltimore: Penguin, 1958), p. 287.

A contemporary version of this perspective has been proposed by Eleonore Stump, "The Problem of Evil," *Faith and Philosophy* 2, no. 4 (October 1985): 392-423.

[12]A version of this perspective can be found in Thomas Tracy, "Victimization and the Problem of Evil: A Response to Ivan Karamazov," *Faith and Philosophy* 9, no. 3 (1992): pp. 301-19. See also John Hick, *Evil and the God of Love* (London: Macmillan, 1966; rev. ed. 1978).

[13]This principle is defended, for example, by Yandell in "Greater Good Defense."

[14]A variation of this defense of the coherence of (M4) first appeared in David

Basinger, "In What Sense Must God Be Omnibenevolent?" *International Journal for the Philosophy of Religion* 14 (1983): 5-8.

[15]John D. Arras and Bonnie Steinbock, *Ethical Issues in Modern Medicine*, 4th ed. (Mountain View, Calif.: Mayfield, 1995), p. 12.

[16]Robert Adams, "Must God Create the Best?" *Philosophical Review* 81 (1972), reprinted in *The Concept of God*, ed. Thomas V. Morris (New York: Oxford University Press, 1987), pp. 91-106 (future references from this latter source); "Existence, Self-Interest and the Problem of Evil," *Nous* 13 (1979): 53-65.

[17]Adams acknowledges that "given the apparent unhappiness of some people's lives," recompense in an afterlife may be necessary in some cases to ensure an existence that is on the whole worth living ("Existence, Self-Interest and the Problem of Evil," p. 56). All of his examples, though, are limited to our *earthly* existence.

[18]See pp. 62, 66-67 in this chapter for a fuller discussion of this point.

[19]Adams, "Must God Create the Best?" pp. 92-93.

[20]Adams, "Existence, Self-Interest and the Problem of Evil," pp. 53-56.

[21]Ibid., pp. 54-55, 64.

[22]Ibid., p. 60.

[23]Adams, "Must God Create the Best?" pp. 97-98.

[24]My critique of Adams is a variation of what first appeared in "In What Sense Must God Be Omnibenevolent?" pp. 8-15.

[25]William Hasker, "Must God Do His Best?" *International Journal for Philosophy of Religion* 16 (1984): 213-23.

[26]Ibid., pp. 214-15.

[27]Ibid., pp. 216-17.

[28]Ibid., p. 216.

[29]George Schlesinger, "Omnipotence and Evil: An Incoherent Problem," *Sophia* 4 (1965): 21.

[30]George Schlesinger, "The Problem of Evil and the Problem of Suffering," *American Philosophical Quarterly* 1 (July 1964): 244.

[31]Hasker, "Must God Do His Best?" pp. 218-19.

[32]This response to Hasker first appeared (in slightly altered form) in my "In What Sense Must God Do His Best? A Response to Hasker," *International Journal for the Philosophy of Religion* 18 (1985): 161-64.

Chapter 4: Basic Freewill Theism & Evil

[1]See chapter one, pp. 32-36, for a description of basic freewill theism (BFWT).

[2]See David and Randall Basinger, "The Problem with the 'Problem of Evil,' " *Religious Studies* 30 (1994): 89-97.

[3]See, for example, John Feinberg, *The Many Faces of Evil* (Grand Rapids, Mich.: Zondervan, 1994), chap. 1; David Griffin, *Evil Revisited: Responses and Reconsiderations* (Albany: State University of New York Press, 1991); William Hasker, *God, Time and Knowledge* (Ithaca, N.Y.: Cornell University Press,

1989), chap. 10.

[4]Michael Peterson, *Evil and the Christian God* (Grand Rapids, Mich.: Baker Book House, 1982), p. 19.

[5]To say that a state of affairs, *S*, has intrinsic negative value in any given world, *W*, is to say in simplest terms that *W* would have been better off without *S*.

[6]See Feinberg, *Many Faces of Evil*, chap. 11, for a good discussion of the ambiguity surrounding these terms.

[7]Those who believe that God possesses middle knowledge deny that God, *before creation*, had knowledge of any actualizable world that would have better satisfied his creative goals. Those who believe that God possesses only present knowledge or simple foreknowledge deny that God, *since creation*, has ever had such knowledge. See chapter two.

[8]The clearest discussions of this perspective are found in Hasker, *God, Time and Knowledge*, chap. 10; Peterson, *Evil and the Christian God*; Bruce Reichenbach, *Evil and a Good God* (New York: Fordham University Press, 1982); Richard Swinburne, *The Existence of God* (Oxford: Clarendon, 1979), chaps. 10-11.

[9]See, for instance, Peterson, *Evil and the Christian God*, pp. 17-18.

[10]Alvin Plantinga, "Reply to the Basingers on Divine Omnipotence," *Process Studies* 11, no. 1 (1981): 26-27.

[11]This is not to say that Plantinga is not a freewill theist, but only that he has not chosen to discuss the "truth" of those beliefs that freewill theists hold.

[12]William Hasker makes this claim in "A Philosophical Perspective," in Clark Pinnock et al., *The Openness of God: A Biblical Challenge to the Traditional Understanding of God* (Downers Grove, Ill.: InterVarsity Press, 1994), pp. 126-54, and in *God, Time and Knowledge*, chap. 10. In neither source does he explicitly state that he is discussing freewill theists. But he has in mind those theists who are proponents of what I am labeling BFWT, and therefore I believe it appropriate in this context to couch his comments in these terms.

[13]Hasker, "Philosophical Perspective," pp. 146-47.

[14]Ibid., p. 152.

[15]Hasker, *God, Time and Knowledge*, p. 204.

[16]Hasker, "Philosophical Perspective," p. 152.

[17]This argument is obviously similar in some ways to Hasker's argument (discussed in chapter three) against the contention that a perfectly good God must do all he can to maximize the quality of life for each individual. In both cases Hasker claims that if a theist maintains that God possesses a certain property (a certain form of divine goodness in chapter three and a certain form of divine knowledge in this chapter), then this theist must also maintain that God possesses meticulous providence and that this has undesirable consequences.

This argument is also directly related to Hasker's argument (discussed in chapter two) against the contention that a freewill theist can justifiably maintain that God possesses MK. In both cases Hasker claims that a God with MK possesses too much power over earthly affairs (in chapter two too much power to be the risk-taker that the God of BFWT must be, and in this chapter too much power to be able to offer a plausible response to evil).

[18]See chapter two, pp. 43-48, for a fuller discussion of this point.

[19]See my "Divine Omniscience and the Soteriological Problem of Evil: Is the Type of Knowledge God Possesses Relevant?" *Religious Studies* 28 (1992): 16-17, for an application of this principle to the eternal destiny of those who have never heard the gospel.

[20]My basic critique of Hasker's argument is similar to my critique of the distinct but related arguments discussed in chapters two and three. In all three cases I deny that a God with MK possesses as much control over earthly affairs as Hasker claims.

[21]William Alston, "The Inductive Argument from Evil and the Human Cognitive Condition," *Philosophical Perspectives* 5 (1991): 29.

[22]This type of challenge is normally labeled the inductive or evidential or empirical or probabilistic problem of evil. See Peterson, *Evil and the Christian God*, chaps. 3-4, and Feinberg, *Many Faces of Evil*, chaps. 8-12, for comprehensive overviews of this approach to the issue.

[23]Richard Swinburne, *The Existence of God* (Oxford: Clarendon, 1979), pp. 254-71. See also Stephen Wykstra, "The Human Obstacle to Evidential Arguments from Suffering: On Avoiding the Evils of 'Appearance,' " *International Journal for Philosophy of Religion* 16 (1984): 83-84.

[24]David Ray Griffin, *God, Power and Evil: A Process Theodicy* (Philadelphia: Westminster Press, 1976), p. 271.

[25]A forceful version of this challenge leveled explicitly against freewill theists can be found in Griffin, *Evil Revisited*, pp. 87-89. A version of this challenge leveled explicitly against those freewill theists who maintain that God possesses MK can be found in Hasker, "Philosophical Perspective." A version`of this challenge leveled against all theists who believe God to be omnipotent and perfectly good can be found in William L. Rowe, "Ruminations About Evil," *Philosophical Perspectives* 5 (1991): 69-87.

[26]William L. Rowe, *Philosophy of Religion* (Encino, Calif.: Dickenson, 1978), p. 89.

[27]Ibid., p. 12.

[28]See, for example, James W. Cornman and Keith Lehrer, *Philosophical Problems and Arguments: An Introduction* (New York: Macmillan, 1970), pp. 340-41. One of the most forceful versions of this argument leveled explicitly against freewill theists appears in Griffin, *Evil Revisited*, pp. 17-19, 91-92. Rowe also argues in this fashion at times, although he does not explicitly distinguish his functional and moral criticisms. See, for instance, his "Ruminations About Evil," p. 72. An interesting variation of this criticism leveled against those freewill theists who believe God possesses MK can be found in David

P. Hunt, "Middle Knowledge and the Soteriological Problem of Evil," *Religious Studies* 27 (March 1991): 3-26.

[29]Alvin Plantinga, "Epistemic Probability and Evil," *Archivio di Filosofia* 56 (1988): 561.

[30]Other examples of this line of reasoning can be found in Wykstra, "Human Obstacle," pp. 73-93, and Garth L. Hallett, "Evil and Human Understanding," *Heythrop Journal* 32 (1991): 467-68.

[31]See, for example, Bruce Reichenbach, "Natural Evils and Natural Laws: A Theodicy for Natural Evils," *International Philosophical Quarterly* 16 (June 1976): 179-96; Swinburne, *Existence of God*, chaps. 10-11; David and Randall Basinger, "Divine Omnipotence: Plantinga vs. Griffin," *Process Studies* 11 (Spring 1981): 11-24.

[32]See, for example, William Hasker, "The Necessity of Gratuitous Evil," *Faith and Philosophy* 9, no. 1 (January 1992): 23-44. Swinburne emphasizes the necessity of natural evil for this purpose in *Existence of God*.

[33]See John Hick, *Evil and the God of Love* (London: Macmillan, 1966).

[34]For discussions of this response, see my "Divine Omniscience and the Soteriological Problem of Evil," pp. 11-12, and my "Process Theism Versus Free-Will Theism: A Response to Griffin," *Process Studies* 20, no. 4 (1991): 209-10. Again see Swinburne, *Existence of God*, chap. 11.

[35]Process theist David Griffin disagrees. (6) can justifiably be rejected, he maintains, only if there exists some plausible reason to believe that a being with the acknowledged characteristics of the God of BFWT would not do more to rid the world of evil. But to be considered plausible a contention must be "psychologically convincing to thoughtful men and women," and no freewill theist, he argues, has yet to offer an explanation for evil that satisfies this requirement. Thus (6) must be affirmed. See Griffin, *Evil Revisited*, p. 89.

However, this will not do. First, it is difficult to see how Griffin could demonstrate in a nonquestion-begging manner that most, or even the majority of, "knowledgeable," "objective," "morally sensitive" individuals actually agree with his contention that the God of BFWT could do more. Moreover, even if this could be established, it would not necessarily follow that freewill theists could not justifiably deny that the type of evil we experience stands as prima facie evidence against God's existence. To establish his point, Griffin must demonstrate that the reasoning of those who reject (6) is inadequate—that those who reject (6) have no justifiable epistemic basis for doing so. But to my knowledge neither Griffin nor any other proponent of (6) has accomplished this task.

[36]C. Stephen Evans, *Philosophy of Religion* (Downers Grove, Ill.: InterVarsity Press, 1985), p. 139. See also Terry Christlieb, "Which Theisms Face an Evidential Problem of Evil?" *Faith and Philosophy* 9, no. 1 (January 1992): 45-64.

[37]See Peterson, *Evil and the Christian God*, chap. 1.

[38]Even Alvin Plantinga, who argues that belief can be properly basic (need not be based on propositional evidence of any sort), acknowledges that we must defeat alleged defeaters of our beliefs. See, for example, Plantinga's "The Foundations of Theism: A Reply," *Faith and Philosophy* 3 (1986): 298-313.

[39]See, for example, Basil Mitchell, "Theology and Falsification," in *New Essays in Philosophical Theology*, ed. Antony Flew and Alasdair MacIntyre (New York: Macmillan, 1955), pp. 103-5; Christlieb, "Which Theisms Face an Evidential Problem of Evil?"

[40]William Rowe, "The Problem of Evil and Some Varieties of Atheism," *American Philosophical Quarterly* 16 (October 1979): 339-40.

[41]Michael Martin, "Is Evil Evidence Against the Existence of God?" *Mind* 87 (1978): 430.

[42]A more extensive critique of Martin's position can be found in my "Evil as Evidence Against God's Existence: Some Clarifications," *The Modern Schoolman* 58 (1981): 175-84.

[43]Swinburne, *Existence of God*, p. 220.

[44]See also Alvin Plantinga, "The Probabilistic Argument from Evil," *Philosophical Studies* 35, no. 1 (January 1979): 1-53. It is important to state explicitly what I am here denying. I am not denying that there exist neutral criteria that allow us to maintain that belief in God is justified, given evil. I am denying that there exist neutral criteria that allow us to maintain that belief (or disbelief) in God is *not* justified, given evil.

Chapter 5: Basic Freewill Theism & Petitionary Prayer

[1]Some theists also believe that our prayers can, apart from God, directly affect even those who are not consciously aware of the fact that petitions are being offered on their behalf. See, for example, Frank Laubach, *Prayer: The Mightiest Force in the World* (Old Tappan, N.J.: Revell, 1959); Marjorie Suchocki, "A Process Theology of Prayer," *American Journal of Theology and Philosophy* 2 (May 1981).

[2]See chapter one, pp. 27-29, for a more thorough discussion of theological determinism.

[3]*Summa Theologiae* 1a.19.8.

[4]See chapter one, pp. 22-23, for a more thorough introduction to process thought.

[5]See Suchocki, "Process Theology of Prayer."

[6]The question of why God does not utilize this power to prevent more evil is discussed in chapter four.

[7]See chapter one, pp. 34-36.

[8]This characterization of the potential efficacy of petitionary prayer for these three perspectives is a modified, abridged version of what first appeared in David Basinger, "Practical Implications," in Clark Pinnock et al., *The Openness of God: A Biblical Challenge to the Traditional Understanding of God* (Down-

ers Grove, Ill.: InterVarsity Press, 1994), pp. 156-62.

[9]Michael J. Murray and Kurt Meyers, "Ask and It Will Be Given to You," *Religious Studies* 30 (1994): 311-30.

[10]Ibid., p. 319.

[11]Ibid.

[12]Ibid. A somewhat analogous line of reasoning can also be found in the writings of Martin Luther. "God did not command prayer in order to deceive you and make a fool, a monkey out of you; he wants you to pray and to be confident that you will be heard. You must present your need to God . . . in order that you may learn to know yourself, where you are lacking." *Martin Luther: Selections from His Writings*, ed. John Dillenberger (Garden City, N.Y.: Anchor/Doubleday, 1961), p. 217.

[13]I am assuming that when Murray and Meyers make reference to *God's will* in this context, they are referring to what *God values* or that which is consistent with *God's moral nature*. So I will use these terms interchangeably.

[14]Murray and Meyers, "Ask and It Will Be Given to You," p. 320. To state this important point differently, the model in question is helpful only if believers can know with some degree of certainty that "an event of one sort or another happened (or failed to happen) as a result of their petition" (p. 321). But given the various reasons why a believer may or may not receive that which has been requested, can the petitioner have any such assurance?

[15]Ibid., pp. 321-22.

[16]This critique of Murray and Meyers's position first appeared in my "Petitionary Prayer: A Response to Murray and Meyers," *Religious Studies* 31 (1995): 475-84.

[17]Eleonore Stump, "Petitionary Prayer," *American Philosophical Quarterly* 16 (April 1979): 81-91. Reprinted in *Miracles*, ed. Richard Swinburne (New York: Macmillan, 1989), pp. 167-88; all subsequent references are to this source.

[18]This illustration is not explicitly found in Stump's discussion but is consistent with it.

[19]Stump, "Petitionary Prayer," p. 180. In an analogous manner, Vincent Brummer notes that if God did not in some cases provide for us only upon request, our relationship with God would become depersonalized in the sense that we would have no need to share our desires with him. See *What Are We Doing When We Pray?* (London: SCM Press, 1984), p. 47.

[20]This is especially true for proponents of BFWT, who believe that God desires a world in which individuals possess significant moral autonomy.

[21]Stump explicitly discusses a related problem: whether it would be fair to a person to receive *uninvited* help primarily because this help was requested by a friend. Cannot the person giving the help (e.g., a teacher or God) be accused of meddling in this case? He or she can, Stump believes, to the extent that the person needing help has not freely shared his problem with the person asking for the help. The most a teacher can do is "to try to elicit from

[the student needing help] in genuinely noncoercive ways a request for help." And likewise, she maintains, God can avoid the charge of oppressive meddling only if the person God has been asked to help comes to the place where he "has willingly shared his thoughts and feelings and the like with God." Stump, "Petitionary Prayer," pp. 182-83.

[22]In some religious circles to pray for such things is sinful.

[23]R. T. Allen, "On Not Understanding Prayer," *Sophia* 11 (1972): 2.

[24]Murray and Meyers, "Ask and It Will Be Given to You," pp. 313-14. A very similar line of reasoning is offered by John Calvin: "Prayer is not so much for his sake as for ours. . . . It is very much for our interest to be constantly supplicating him: first, that our heart may be always inflamed with a serious and ardent desire for seeking, loving and serving him, while we accustom ourselves to have recourse to him as a sacred anchor in every necessity; secondly, that no desire, no longing whatever, of which we are ashamed to make him the witness, may enter our minds, while we learn to place all our wishes in his sight, and thus pour out our heart before him; and lastly, that we may be prepared to receive all his benefits with true gratitude and thanksgiving, while our prayers remind us that they proceed from his hand." *Institutes of the Christian Religion*, trans. Henry Beveridge II (Grand Rapids, Mich.: Eerdmans, 1979), p. 147.

[25]See chapter three.

[26]In seeming response to this sort of moral consideration, Stump acknowledges that God might ultimately perform those beneficial acts he desires to perform, even if not requested to do so, but (1) "not in the same amount of time or not by the same process or not with the same effect" or (2) "at the expense of the good wrought and preserved by petitionary prayer." Perhaps God, she suggests, would have brought it about that Augustine was converted even if his mother had not prayed, but not in such a way that he became one of the most powerful Christian authorities. Stump, "Petitionary Prayer," pp. 184, 187.

[27]We must distinguish this moral principle from one requiring only that God ensure (or attempt to ensure) that our lives, considering both our earthly experiences and that which we might experience in an afterlife, will on the whole be satisfying. Given this latter principle, God obviously has much greater leeway with respect to how he interacts with us now. Again, see chapter three.

[28]Robert Adams, "Must God Create the Best?" *Philosophical Review* 81 (1972); reprinted in *The Concept of God*, ed. Thomas V. Morris (New York: Oxford University Press, 1987), pp. 91-106 (quote from p. 96).

[29]See chapter three, pp. 62, 66-67, 70, for a fuller discussion of this point.

[30]Of course a God with MK would know exactly how the withholding of a basic provision would affect the overall quality of life of the individual(s) in question, so the claim here is not that a being with such knowledge would

inadvertently violate the moral principle in question. The claim is simply that given all the factors that tend already to make the lives of many individuals not on the whole worth living (at least from their perspective), it is questionable whether God could honor his commitment to the principle in question if he withheld basic provisions even occasionally.
[31]See chapter three.

Appendix
[1]David P. Hunt, "Divine Providence and Simple Foreknowledge," *Faith and Philosophy* 10, no. 3 (July 1993): 394-414.
[2]David Basinger, "Simple Foreknowledge and Providential Control," *Faith and Philosophy* 10, no. 3 (July 1993): 421-27.
[3]David P. Hunt, "Prescience and Providence: A Reply to My Critics," *Faith and Philosophy* 10, no. 3 (July 1993): 433-34.
[4]See chapter three, pp. 59-60, for an expanded discussion of this point.
[5]We have already seen as a general principle that God can benefit providentially only if his foreknowledge is limited (selective, partial). Therefore it should not surprise us that the model in question will "work" only if we attempt to limit functionally God's foreknowledge, while still maintaining that he possesses it.
[6]Hunt, "Divine Providence," p. 436.
[7]Ibid., p. 437.
[8]Hunt also argues that I have erred at this point by being too specific. "God's conditional decisions," he tells us, "are reached logically prior to the actualization of a particular world, and thus must contain general terms rather than proper names." But once we have replaced specific statements about Sue and Tom with generalized statements about individuals with certain properties, he maintains, (C3) can retain providential efficacy while avoiding my criticism (ibid., p. 436).

I deny, however, that God's conditional decisions must contain only general terms. Moreover, even if we assume that God's response to Sue could justifiably be triggered by generalized antecedent conditionals that do not include any specific information about her, it still remains true in any world, W, in which Sue (or any specific woman) asks God at time $t1$ whether she should marry Tom (or any specific man) that a God with complete SFK will know (among other things) at $t1$ in W whether Sue (or any other specific woman) will refuse or accept Tom's (or any other man's) proposal and whether what is best will or will not come about as a result. Thus a "generalized" (C3) remains subject to exactly the same line of criticism that Hunt had hoped to avoid.
[9]Hunt disagrees, arguing that this line of reasoning involves me in yet another fatalistic fallacy. "The fact that Sue does not refuse Tom's proposal does not make it providentially irrelevant that, *were* Sue to refuse his

proposal, what is best for her would probably come about (indeed, if Sue accepts the proposal, it may be because God refrained from advising her against it). So, if [it is true that Sue would probably benefit if she refuses Tom's proposal], then whether or not Sue refuses (and God *knows* she refuses), God has the power, through advising Sue against marriage, to bring about conditions in which the achievement of his providential ends is more likely. What more is required for God's foreknowledge of Tom's death to be providentially useful?" (ibid., pp. 435-36).

I certainly do not deny that there could be worlds in which "Sue accepts the proposal . . . because God refrained from advising her against it." But we are not at present concerned with such worlds. The question at hand is whether the implementation of (C3)—that is, whether an attempt on God's part to convince Sue to refuse Tom's proposal, in a world in which we know Sue beneficially (or nonbeneficially) accepts the proposal—could make the achievement of his providential ends more likely. And I do not see anything in Hunt's comments that justifies the belief that an attempt on God's part to convince Sue to refuse the proposal can increase the likelihood that his ends will be achieved in this context *because of what he foreknows about Tom*.

[10]We could, of course, circumvent the problems that beset (C3) by excluding from the relevant conditional even beliefs about how Sue will respond to Tom's death. But this would generate an equally serious difficulty. If there is nothing in the antecedent conditions of God's decision that indicates how Sue responds to Tom's death if she accepts or rejects his proposal, then again the implementation of such a decision can in no sense increase God's ability to bring about his desired end.

[11]Hunt, "Divine Providence," pp. 437-38.

[12]Ibid., p. 437.

[13]See chapter two, pp. 39-40, 49-52, for a fuller discussion of present knowledge.